# AT WAR WITH POLITICS

Dr Stephen Graves

# AT WAR WITH POLITICS

# A Journey from Traditional Political Science to Black Politics

## The Black Studies Collection

Collection editor
**Dr Christopher McAuley**

To my brother YaKima Donnell Ward.

To Arpad Kadarkay, AT, Otty, Krohn, Pitre, Robert Ostergard, Luqman, K Lynn, Arthur, Ben, and my wonderful parents and children who gave me everything I needed to be who I am.

First published in 2023 by Lived Places Publishing

The authors and editors have made every effort to ensure the accuracy of information contained in this publication, but assumes no responsibility for any errors, inaccuracies, inconsistencies and omissions. Likewise, every effort has been made to contact copyright holders. If any copyright material has been reproduced unwittingly and without permission the Publisher will gladly receive information enabling them to rectify any error or omission in subsequent editions.

British Library Cataloguing in Publication Data
A CIP record for this book is available from the British Library

ISBN: 978-1-915271-09-9 (pbk)
ISBN: 978-1-915271-11-2 (ePDF)
ISBN: 978-1-915271-10-5 (ePUB)

The right of Stephen Graves to be identified as the Author of this work has been asserted by them in accordance with the Copyright, Design and Patents Act 1988.

Cover design by Fiachra McCarthy
Book design by Rachel Trolove of Twin Trail Design
Typeset by Newgen Publishing UK

Lived Places Publishing
Long Island
New York 11789

www.livedplacespublishing.com

# Abstract

By reflecting on his own background and educational experiences, political scientist Stephen Graves, PhD explores the relationship between his career path and his own identity. Graves employs a personal lens to investigate the journey of a Black scholar looking for the best way to make changes in his community. His collegiate career studying politics is defined by challenging major themes in American government while the political issues he identifies as important to Black communities are invisible among the academic discourse he encounters. With seemingly no clear political home to find himself, he turns to political philosophy and discovers his own brand of Black politics. Mixing political philosophy and Black studies, Graves employs a personal lens that ultimately empowers him throughout his education and into his future. Ultimately finding a career in teaching provided the opportunity to engage students pursuing their own paths and identities in politics, while hoping to be agents of change.

## Key words

African American; Black politics; political science; autobiography; philosophy; political theory; American government; higher education; racism

# Content warning

These content notes are made available so that readers can be informed and be aware of the specific wording found in this book. Some readers might find some language and themes triggering. For example:

- Uncensored use of the n-word
- The theme that some people are better than others, although not naturally or due to physical appearance, strength, or wealth, but due to their beliefs, ideas, and willpower

I hope that you will find the use of this content valuable in telling this particular story about specific moments in time.

# A note on language

The capitalization of Black is standard practice in leading style guides such as *The Chicago Manual of Style* and *The Diversity Style Guide*. For many people, Black reflects a shared sense of identity and community. White carries a different set of meanings, thus, capitalizing "white" in this context risks following the lead of white supremacists.

This work employs a common Afro American vernacular when referring to particular ethnic groups as "Blacks" and "whites."

# Contents

# Learning objectives

The text inspires an interdisciplinary literary review of several related bodies of theory about the diversity of the Black lived experience. Focusing on the central topic of resilience in the face of adversity while searching not only for an identity, but a career, consider:

- What is the impact of structural racism on the ability for self-identifying?
- Is the pursuit of truth compatible with the acquisition of the American Dream?
- Are current academic viewpoints about fear, hate, compassion, and success in need of a post-COVID-19 reevaluation?

# Preface

Throughout my career I have kept many of the books, notes, and notepads going back to my undergraduate days. Many of the books that currently sit on my shelf have survived the journey with me for over 20 years. The ideas and papers that I wrote are still accessible and I still go through them. Part of what made this project what it has become is the ability to experience the evolution of those ideas over time, from an angry 18-year-old, first-time college student to a teacher writing about the same topics and concepts I did as a teenager. Having access to my earliest thoughts and ideas was important. Although some of these ideas may be troublesome for some to read, I can assure you they are expressed with the greatest intent for the common good.

When I was first approached about doing this project, the first question I asked was, "how honest can I be?" In instances where I am speaking or writing about myself, my strategy has always been to be as honest and authentic as possible or allowed. The academic journey was not difficult for me to write about. It has never been difficult for me to talk about. I have shared it with my students many times over the years. I find nothing in my thought processes or experiences as a student to be anything to be ashamed about or ashamed to share. As in life, the journey often gets muddy, uncomfortable, and sometimes dark. Over the years, my reflections over my academic career have brought me a great sense of joy. I have always felt that if my story can help one student succeed, then I would regard it as a success. I was once that one student.

There is a lot to be said about the human condition and how I learned to navigate through life with what appeared to me at the time was constant disappointment and suffering. I learned a lot not only about myself, but also about my surroundings and the different types of people I encountered: across the economic spectrum, all races, levels of education, and ages. As much as people were different, there were consistent themes and behaviors that I witnessed. Part of theorizing and philosophizing about politics is making generalizations, in particular about the human condition. As much as people want to be different and express their individuality, there are certain elements that hold true across the human condition. We all want safety, to be healthy, and for opportunities to be successful. Yet, we all deal differently with the obstacles and adversity we face in acquiring these things. It is not so much what we want out of life as much as it is how we all envision ourselves getting there. There is no doubt that I did not envision my career in politics or education going the way it does in these pages. And yet, by writing this book, I could not imagine it going any other way.

# Introduction

Growing up, I would have never thought for a day that I would be a teacher. I thought I would go to college but never imagined I would get a degree in political science. My earliest hopes and dreams involved playing college sports on my way to being a professional athlete or being a child star on Nickelodeon or on the Mickey Mouse Club. As children, my brothers and I used to sing and dance in our mother's living room like the Jacksons or New Edition. I had little knowledge or understanding of politics. My parents never talked about political parties or candidates, and I did not know any Black teachers as a child. The first Black teacher I ever had was a substitute named Mr Walden. When I was in sixth grade I had my first full-time Black teacher, Ms Williams. She was the first teacher that could get me to quit being a class clown and my mom picked her out specifically, even pulling me out of the class I was in and physically walking me to the principal and telling her to put me in Ms Williams's class. The journey into a career in teaching was unexpected and full of trials and tribulations. To be teaching political science is startling, even to me.

Writing this book definitely brought back many memories and thoughts about my overall experience in academia and working in politics. While many could not be shared, I certainly did my best to be as authentic and genuine as possible. So why would I write a book about my lived experiences en route to becoming a professor? First, I do not think that this story is all that original or unique to my particular experience alone. Sometimes it seems like people are in such a hurry to be different and express their individuality that they forget that there are millions of people out there who are quite possibly going through many of the same challenges. There is a sense of comfort that soothes a spirit when it feels like it isn't the only one suffering. There are millions of kids going through high school and college right now, trying to find themselves and discover what they believe in or what they want to be. If my journey is able to assist anyone out there who is going through a similar journey, or even considering it, then I will feel accomplished.

Second, I see a lot of myself in the trials and frustrations of the Black students who currently major in political science. A lot of students ask me, "how the hell did you end up in politics?" There is a lot in traditional political science that turns Black people off. There is a lot in the practice of politics that turns Black people off: its history of racism and white supremacy, the inadequacies in America's election system, and the sheer lack of representation of Black people in political science careers, not just in teaching it. Yet, not having a Black face in the classroom to help navigate very important topics that frame our existence in this country can be problematic and traumatizing. I hear Black students' stories of the comments made by their white peers, emboldened by their majority status and the lack of courage by professors to thwart the continued ignorance that many white students perpetuate. I teach Black students who are living in a constant state of having to defend themselves and their community publicly in front of their white peers. The tradition of political science has devolved into a discipline with very little social value in a nation that currently is dealing with political chaos. Black people in the US are also looking for ways to explain the political trappings they consistently encounter, and they are looking for answers to dismantle the institutional racism that permeates the nation. If progress is to ever take place in the US, I do believe it will take a change in the way we study and learn about politics. Better yet, how we come to understand politics.

There are many important themes and concepts that help frame this work, including Black identity and political identity. The role that a person's identification plays in their confidence and mental well-being is an important element of Black identity. Identities are first and foremost adopted to serve basic needs such as autonomy and to manage relations (Ryan & Deci, 2003). Identification serves to increase a person's feelings of worth and importance by exhibiting values or characteristics that are well-received by others. There are two main dimensions in which a person's identity plays out: internal and external. Internal dimensions refer to inherent, genetic attributes over which the individual has no control, such as color or ancestry. External dimensions are those based on political, social, and economic forces including certain cultural phenomena. A Black identity is described as an individual and collective conscious effort by people of African descent to be self-naming and self-defining as a means to increase the human respect and dignity of African people and their descendants (Claybook, 2021). The socio-historical and political context of the 1960s redefined and recreated what it meant to be Black in America. One of the biggest factors that contributes to Black identity is the belief that Africans have their own ontology or concept of universal reality. The psychological foundation of this distinct and unique concept of reality traces its beginnings back to ancient Kemet civilization around 3200 BC. Since I attended predominately white institutions until I attended Howard University, a premier historically Black college (HBCU) located in Washington, DC, much of my academic and educational experience is centered on investigating and exploring my own Black identity and the challenges in doing so.

Not only did my Black identity evolve, but I was additionally tasked with learning about and forming a political identity. Political identities refer to identification with and meaning attributed to membership in politically relevant groups, including political parties and national, ethnic, linguistic, or gender groups (Huddy, 2013). There is an important functional element to political identity, insofar as it plays an important role in sustaining a person's allegiance and loyalty to their political community. For example, research has shown that individuals who strongly identify with their group are more likely to act on behalf of group-related causes, to view the political environment in antagonistic terms, and to act defensively in the face of group criticism. Thus, my exploration into Black identity became consequentially aligned with my political identity. I almost immediately associated my political beliefs with Black culture and the injustices experienced by Black people in the US. Black politics was life. And it was everywhere.

Politically, Black identity provides Black people with a racialized political identity around which to mobilize and organize. For Black Americans, who view the US as a racialized environment, redefining one's individual and collective racialized identity, from one of shame and humiliation due to the history of slavery and racism, to one of affirmation and pride is a form of resistance. Black activists in the 1960s constructed a positive and reaffirming racialized identity developed out of a shared history of experiences for people of African descent. Material conditions and the lived experiences of struggling against exploitative and racist conditions shape and reshape Black identities. People of African descent continue to shape their identities by their resistance to and transformative efforts against racist institutions and societal practices. Their retention of their African culture, which is empowering, as well as shared experiences with racism, which are oppressive, represent the arena in which their identity is forged. A Black identity is political in its struggle against racist power dynamics and structures. A strong sense of Black identity is threatened by the constant repression that many Black people face in predominately white institutions.

Consequently, much of the material that makes up this lived experience is contained within this contentious contest of looking for an identity that is negatively perceived in one's immediate environment. In many instances, this experience can lead to a disconnect from Blackness that many Black students have expressed to me. By disconnected, I mean an identity that appears to be separate from someone or not fitting well together or understanding each other. I would later come to understand this concept as alienation. Being disconnected in the context of this lived experience also includes lack of access to a clear, uninterrupted version of one's Black identity. For many in poor, Black communities, there are limitations to what we have access to that resembles and expresses our identities, thus, what little we may interact with in predominately white places and spaces is compromised by what we have access to. In many instances, these are not the most empowering images and representations of that. This happens a lot within the discipline of political science which has few major Black figures, both in its American setting and in its institutional practices. My experience in Black politics focused on combining my identity with what I was learning. Thus, one of the major relationships that the lived experience in this text highlights is racial unity. Racial unity, in particular for Black Americans who represent a numerical and political minority, has social, political, and economic implications. In electoral politics, Black voters use the group's well-being as a proxy for their own interests, which some have labeled the "Black utility heuristic" (Wamba, 1999). Other studies suggest racial identity and social pressure shape Blacks into an electoral monolith. The idea is that Blacks vote similarly as a show of racial solidarity.

Another explanation is that, despite their ideological diversity, Black voters prioritize civil rights issues. Essentially, the polarized civil rights stances of the parties have turned Blacks into single-issue voters. This results in Blacks being a "captured minority," wherein they have no viable alternative to the Democratic Party. Much of the Black political experience in America, especially in its contemporary context, starts and begins with the Democratic Party. The modern Democratic Party is associated with progressive causes, like welfare and universal health care, that are perceived to be of more central importance to Black Americans. Over half of Black Americans surveyed in 2016 believed that the economy was getting worse, and over 40 percent believed that Blacks were falling behind economically. Since then, only one in ten Black voters in the survey believed that Black people are getting ahead economically, and that sentiment holds broadly across age and education groups. Over three-quarters of all Black voters believe the country is generally heading in the wrong direction (Newkirk, 2018). Eighty-nine percent of Black voters believe racism in the country has gotten worse since 2016, the same proportion believes racism is prevalent in America, and over half believe that one of the key shifts in American politics has been a renewed attack on Black Americans. Even when a Black electorate has the choice between two African American candidates, with one candidate running as a Republican who emphasizes traditional values, and the competing candidate running as a Democrat who supports gay marriage and abortion, the Democrat still wins the majority of African American votes (Kidd et al., 2007). Authors have found that despite the Republican candidate's highlighted support of issues important to African Americans, the Democratic label had more of an effect on African American voting behavior. Although the social issues highlighted in the election such as abortion and gay marriage were important to African Americans, they were not issues central to African Americans as a group. It is with the backdrop of this history that I explore my own political realities and how I would approach my education in political science.

Last, there are the concepts of politics and "politicking." Politics is the process that determines what government does and it is an important theme within these pages. It comprises all the activities of cooperation, negotiation, and conflict within and between individuals, groups, and cultures, whereby people go about organizing the use, production, or distribution of human, natural, and other resources in the course of the production and reproduction of their biological and social lives (Leftwich, 2004). Politicking is the performative aspect of politics and refers to the tactics needed to acquire or retain the power of politics itself (Palonen, 2003). Government is the system by which decisions are implemented through the political process. The role of government is to arguably serve two broad purposes: to provide order and to promote general welfare.

The final major concept that guides this lived experience is political ideology. A political ideology represents a cohesive set of ideas and beliefs used to organize and evaluate the political world and help shape an individual's specific beliefs. Ultimately, it forms the basis for how we perceive the world around us. Political ideologies are associated with power structures. Politicians seek power. Their political ideology and the social, economic, and political circumstances of their time influence what politicians do with that power. The use of power always takes place within the framework of a particular ideology. As a result, modern politics can only be properly understood by reference to the great ideological movements of the modern era: conservatism, liberalism, socialism, nationalism, fascism, and so on.

All of the evidence of racial politics in America points to a unique interplay of economic and racial factors that form a continuum of disadvantage for Black voters. The increasing likelihood of Black voters experiencing racism and seeing it as a major structural impediment is one of the biggest shifts in voter outlook across demographics over the last ten years. Only a quarter of all Black Americans said they did not experience racism in a 2008 Center on African American Politics and Society poll, and Barack Obama's 2008 presidential election that year marked a spike in racial optimism among Black voters. In another poll, across income, geographic, and age groups, Black voters see "fighting to end racism and discrimination" as the most important electoral concern, with school funding, access to affordable health care, and fighting for the poor as the next most important issues. While it might be expected that those issues might continue a natural affinity between Black voters and Democrats, Black voters are increasingly skeptical of the Democratic Party's ability and commitment to racial justice issues, with 40 percent of all Black voters believing that Democrats are no better than Republicans in ending discrimination or protecting Black people from hate crimes, and over half of all Black voters believing that the Democratic Party is no better than the GOP in eliminating voter-suppression laws. Laird et al. (2018) argues that the continued social isolation of Blacks in American society has created spaces and incentives for the emergence of Black political norms. For example, Democratic partisanship has become significantly tied to Black identity in the US (Laird et al., 2018).

All these concepts play a significant role in my lived experience that I chronicle throughout the rest of this book. In many instances I am still learning about politicking and navigating political spaces between America's two-party system. The last few years have certainly seen an increase in white domestic terrorism, so even a promising and unapologetic Black political identity has its disadvantages. Critical race theory is currently under attack in the education system, which aims to make it harder for kids to learn an accurate depiction of Black history and their historical interactions with whites. This will also undoubtedly make it harder for healthier depictions of empowering Black identities to emerge.

# A brief synopsis

This book is organized around three primary themes. The first theme of this book focuses on my student years, from high school until I finished my PhD as a graduate student at Howard University. Chapter 1 identifies my high school and undergraduate days in the Pacific Northwest as most important in the development of my political and intellectual identity. Navigating predominately white institutions and spaces during these years helped shape and mold a particular view of the world. Ultimately, these formative years would set the tone for what would eventually become a career teaching political science and Black studies at university level.

While Chapter 1 sets the foundation of my intellectual pursuits as a student, Chapter 2 will focus primarily on my graduate school experience and the process of putting the foundational tools gathered from my undergraduate studies into a solid research plan. These experiences will also highlight the journey studying political science and many of the problematic concepts and theories that helped guide my research and understanding of American politics and government. My graduate school years were also the first time I entered the classroom as a lecturer and the experiences in teaching early on provided me with a teaching style and philosophy that would prove helpful as my career advanced.

My experiences in US politics outside of academia, including my time spent working in state government and later on in national politics while interning for a trade union, are important elements in the next section. I learned a lot about politics in the classroom, and about politicking while working in local institutional politics.

As Chapter 3 explains, the founding fathers are at the root of the frustration and political disaster that is US politics. What began in college as an awareness of the constant force of white unity surrounding America's founding and the importance given to the legacy of the founding fathers, would later evolve into disdain for a political system and ideological experiment that did more harm to Black people than was admitted, in addition to maintaining a system that allowed for Black suffering and oppression to continue. The struggle with America's fascination with its founding rooted my cause. My problems with US politics and the incompetency of our political institutions starts at the very beginning of this country.

If Chapter 3 highlights the foundational roots of the problems in US politics in theory, Chapter 4 traces the problems and ineffectiveness of US politics by following my government jobs while working my way through school. The contradictory nature of US politics eventually led to me choosing a career in academia. Working in politics at the local and state level undoubtedly had a major influence in my choice of a career as a college professor instead of seeking a career as a politician. Having had an up close and personal look at the inner workings of American politics, this led to a shift in my career aspirations as what I identified with as a young Black male, and later what I knew as a student of politics, became less compatible with electoral politics.

Chapter 5 concludes this book by examining my teaching career in Political Science and eventually Black Studies. What started out as a hopeful career teaching political theory in a political science department would eventually lead me to leaving political science and finding a home in Black Studies, where I was able to put my particular expertise in Black politics to use. Finding a home in Black Studies enabled me to teach what I love: describing and researching the Black political experience. This had always evaded me throughout my academic career, especially as a student in predominately white institutions that saw little to no value in the Black experience overall, let alone in the field of politics where the extent of their political inquiry started at slavery and ended with Martin Luther King, Jr. Ultimately, my trials and experiences as a student, and later as an employee in local government working in politics, put me in the position to be exactly where I needed to be: immersed in the Black political experience.

By no means is this book a tutorial or guide to "becoming a college professor." Many of the experiences that brought me to the point of teaching Black politics I would never recommend another student go through or even, in many cases, try. But there is a lot to be said about a young Black male trying to find his way in a profession that barely sees him and rarely finds his contributions worthwhile. The point of this book is simply to add a word to this extremely important narrative, no matter how small and insignificant it may be in the grand scheme of things. I encounter and interact with students all over the world whom I identify with and can share their frustrations with the educational system and the political climate. I can sense and understand young people trying to find not only a career but also an identity as they venture out into the world for the first time alone. This story of my experiences in this process is shared by millions of Black college students who are continually facing uphill battles in just trying to be great in a world that has consistently portrayed them as less than.

# 1
# The student

## Why politics?

Being a university professor is like being a lifetime student. We are continually learning. Investigating. Theorizing. Experimenting. The thing that separates the younger version of me as a student and the student that I am today is the focus and concentration spent being a student. Now, I have a specialty, an area of concentration that directs the majority of my reading and writing. In my earliest days, my educational pursuits were unfocused experimentation. That all changed when I learned the value of education at the end of my sophomore year of high school. When I say value, I'm really speaking in economic terms at this point. Although a pretty good athlete, I was five-foot-nothing, with my childhood dream of being a professional athlete slowly deteriorating. During my sophomore year, my mother was diagnosed with multiple sclerosis (MS). Both my older brothers had moved out of the home, and it was just my mother and me left. At this point, going to college by any means necessary became my first priority. Prior to then, education was a roller coaster for me. From kindergarten, I was a brilliant, straight-A student in the talented and gifted program (TAG). They pulled me out of my traditional class once a week and had me study and take tests in a separate space. I was the only Black person in the program at my school. Only my mother and I knew about it. It was nothing to be broadcasted to family or friends. As a result, I saw little to no social value in being intelligent. It made me no friends, affected none of my familial or personal relationships, and I still routinely got into trouble and was suspended from school. By the time I was in fifth grade, I was a straight-A student, but I also had an elementary school high of 39 referrals resulting in disciplinary action. This left me only one referral away from being expelled from school. Somehow, some way, I was able to make it through the rest of the school year, and that is due to a lot of generosity. At no point do I believe the fact that I was smart benefited me in any way.

By the time I went to high school, the same pattern had pretty much repeated itself, now, minus the grades in the first two years. Having recognized the lack of social value in being smart, at a moment in time where peer pressure and social value are the highest priority, I settled into class clown-ish ways, doing just enough to remain eligible for sports. My mother was still working two jobs, leaving me mostly self-reliant in regard to my studies. Because there was very little accountability and I knew how to do just enough to remain under the radar, at least academically, I had no problems floating through the first two years of high school. I was a student in name and occupation only.

As previously mentioned, by the end of my sophomore year, my mother's diagnosis resulted in a moment of clarity, ushering me into a feeling of responsibility and leadership that I had not otherwise wanted. I had a small glimpse at the end. It was at that moment I realized that I had to do something BIG. Like it or not, I was going to be responsible. Responsibility was something I was not used to but certainly not unfamiliar with. I remember the last time I saw and spoke to my father before we democratically elected to have him move out of the house. It would be the last time I saw my father in eight years. I walked him to his car after the vote. As we were walking alone, he told me, "Son, take care of your mother. You're the leader of the family now. Family comes first. There is nothing more important than family. You're a king, son. Always remember that." Being the youngest and barely removed from first grade at the time, I saw no point at which his declaration would be true. I had literally no say or impact as the youngest. My brothers were closer in age and were in the same school with the same friends, which left little to no room for me except as entertainment for their friends when needed. Luckily my mother saw the writing on the wall and gave me my own room the first chance she got. This left me to entertain myself in my room when not outside playing with friends. I remember reading every *Goosebumps* and *Encyclopedia Brown* book I could find. *Maniac Magee* was always one of my favorites. Due to the construction of my household, I essentially had no choice but to read and learn in my room. By myself. All day.

When my junior year started, there was still no social value to being smart, especially with the increasing prioritization of socializing. But there was an even bigger practical reason to quit screwing around and focus. I was no longer going to be a professional athlete, so college was going to be the next best thing. My grandfather, father, and my uncle had all been in the military. My father had always told me stories about his time abroad and coming home to all the challenges of racism once he returned. He told stories his father had told him about coming back from war and still not being able to catch a cab home or sit at the front of the train, and how white people had still mistreated him. If I even thought about enrolling in the military, he said he would "personally" kick my ass. The military was not an option. College was my only option. But at this point, I had shown little promise of getting into college. I was an eligible 2.5 student. Average, at best. To get where I needed to be, I had to do something about my grades.

In the last two years of high school, I got straight As back-to-back. I had increased my GPA to above 3.0, was recognized in "Who's Who Among American High School Students," and had assured myself of "getting in somewhere." By no stretch of the imagination would I consider myself a "good" student despite what I had accomplished. Not to diminish the achievement, but I still was not intellectually challenged nor found the social value of education. Getting straight As was not that hard. I could tap into and access that obsessive part of my brain to get good grades. That was apparently all I needed to know at the time. I knew what I was capable of. That was good enough for me.

The high school I attended was predominately white. There was no semblance of Black or African American history and there were no attempts to offer any diversity in the curriculum. I learned little to nothing about Black people. As a student-athlete, being good at sports only acted as a buffer on racial issues. In middle school, I had gotten in fights over the n-word; there were just enough whites, or not enough Blacks, that white students still felt comfortable, and many times defended, using the n-word. There was a feeling among the Black students that being good at sports was the only thing that kept us from a more racially hostile environment. If you were not good at sports, or they had no use for you, then you had no protection from racial backlash. For the most part, I spent my high school career navigating between my predominately white friends while maintaining some semblance of Black identity.

That was until the winter of my senior year. I attended a women's basketball game with my usual group of friends, sitting in our usual spot in the center of the bleachers. During an exchange with a mutual acquaintance, she turned around and called me a "stupid nigger." It just came out of her mouth without hesitation, like she had been saying it her whole life. Nobody said a word. I looked around, not sure what to expect but hoping that someone would say something, anything. But the game and the night carried on. I also said nothing, but I never forgot. But it had finally opened my eyes to the realization of where I was, not only in school, but in society overall. Expendable. No matter the grades, the athletic success, or dating any one of their daughters, I was still Black, and that did not count for much. After that night, I never revisited that situation. I had all the information I needed from the lack of response from being called a "stupid nigger." My Blackness, which had been lying dormant, was now fully activated. My pent-up racial frustration eventually exploded the following MLK Jr holiday. I had found myself roaming the halls in between classes, something that seniors had typically done as we floated through the remainder of our high school careers. One of the students from "leadership," a class focused on spirited assemblies and student engagement, was recording a video about the upcoming holiday and had spotted me coming down the hall. He brought his camera to me and asked me what I thought about the MLK holiday. I immediately launched into a vicious attack on the school and the hypocrisy of celebrating MLK at this predominately white high school that had absolutely no track record of addressing race or racial issues in any impactful way. If anything, they were perpetrators of the racial ignorance that permeated our community. I proceeded to tell him that "everything this school supposedly stands for is shit." At that point, out of the corner of my eye, I had caught the female student who had called me a "stupid nigger" going to her locker. She must have heard my loud tirade about MLK because she turned around to see what all the commotion was about, which at this time I was not trying to contain. The moment we locked eyes, I immediately changed targets. This was an opportunity that was too good to miss. With the camera still rolling, I launched into how she had called me a "nigger" (while pointing to her and saying her name for the camera), and no one had done or said anything. And this was supposed to be one of our best students. A student leader and former class officer. These people had allowed her to call me a "nigger" with no repercussions. "This school is a joke," I went on as I walked off. By the time the bell rang to signal the end of class, the halls had started to fill up, and word had gotten out about my MLK tirade and the calling out of another student. She was upset and crying. I did not care. They wanted me to apologize. I would not. My Black identity had been unleashed.

# College years: the undergraduate

When it came time to choose a college, I wanted to get the best education I could that was not too close to home, where

I could also play football. Although I had given up my dream to be a professional athlete, injuries during high school left me with unfinished business. I decided to attend the University of Puget Sound (UPS) in Tacoma, Washington, about 30 minutes south of Seattle. Puget Sound was a small liberal arts school, predominately white, but heralded itself as the "Harvard of the Northwest." It was a two-hour drive north, the perfect distance for me to be able to drive back and see my family in case of emergency, but far enough that I could reinvent myself. UPS played NCAA Division III football, and I had spent the spring putting together a short highlights video that I sent along with a recruitment form. My mother always told us that if we wanted to go to college, she would do whatever it took. I do not think she meant paying my tuition fees to go to an expensive liberal arts school in another state. But I had dreams of playing college football, and she followed through on putting me through college despite the costs.

In the college's registration booklet for incoming freshmen, there was a list of the majors and programs. I remember my mother saying that before she had kids, she had always planned to go to law school. The most prominent Black figure outside of sports and entertainment was Johnnie Cochran, the lawyer who had just got O. J. Simpson acquitted of murdering his ex-wife. O. J.'s acquittal was monumental for the Black community; whether or not he was innocent or guilty, this was a win for the Black community, and a lot of the reason and praise went to Johnnie Cochran. I decided that if I was going to go to college and wanted the best opportunity to improve not only my own but my family's conditions, then going to law school was going to be my best bet. The closest thing that UPS had was a pre-law program, but there was no pre-law major. I would have to major in something else while being a student in the pre-law program.

One thing I knew for sure: I wanted to learn about Black people (finally!). The only two things that were taught from my K–12 education were slavery and Martin Luther King. That's it. That's the list. I remember watching the movie Malcolm X with my mom and older brothers and wondering who this guy was and how come I had never heard of him. Denzel Washington didn't get the Oscar, but his portrayal of Malcolm X would go down in history. After that movie, the streets were filled with "X" hats and jackets, yet I knew nothing. Throughout high school, Malcolm X had never come up. Ironically, my interest in Black identity, and in what I would later learn to be Black Nationalism, came through the lyrics of the rapper Tupac Shakur. Although he died in 1996 when I was just a freshman in high school, by the time I reached my junior year, his tales about having no friends, squashing his enemies, and "fuck the world" had struck a powerful chord with me. I was initially introduced to 2Pac much earlier. Before the age of ten, my older brothers were playing his Thug Life cassette tapes on our family road trips. I had seen all too much of this "thug life" at home and held some resentment toward it for its role in my confinement to my room during most nights. As a result, I really had no use for it or him. But he was so angry. And I was angry. Until then, my anger had been so internalized, almost crystallized into a state of "woe is me." But in Tupac's lyrics, I heard a message that I had never heard before. He was the first person I ever heard who said that Black people should fight back and that young Black males were trapped in a racist, white man's world. His lyrics mentioned the likes of Malcolm X and the Black Panthers. And almost just as important, Shakur declared that you could be unapologetically pro-Black in any profession, as long as you had enough heart. This was the first time that someone essentially painted a perfect picture of my life and what I was feeling. I had longed to find a focus for my anger. I longed to scream "fuck the world." I just did not know how yet, but I knew I could buy myself some time in college and figure it out.

After being denied so much of Black history prior to college, I noticed the university had an African American Studies department that had a minor but no major. I was now down to my third choice, Politics and Government. It was the closest thing to the law that I could find and seemed to be a worthy fit. These two disciplines seemed to go hand in hand. Thus, I became a Politics and Government major with a minor in African American studies. By the time freshman orientation rolled around for the pre-law program, we had already moved into the dorms. My mom had left to drive back to Portland. We cried like babies in the parking lot. As I made my way to orientation, I was running a few minutes later than I wanted and was walking in just before the meeting was about to start. People were still finding seats under the low murmur of casual introductions and small talk. I scanned the room briefly for anybody I might recognize from moving in or from some other freshman activity from earlier in the day. There was no one. I started to feel uncomfortable standing in the back, looking at this packed room full of pre-law students that only comprised the incoming freshmen. The only seats left were in the back, and I would have to shimmy my way in between people like looking for a seat in the movie theater.

While impatiently scanning the room, I remember thinking to myself, "damn, all these people are pre-law too?" If this was just the incoming freshmen, one could only imagine what the full scale of pre-law students looked like. I had no interest in doing something that everyone else was doing. For a brief second, I had one of those flashbacks you see on television where the star of the show freezes, and a brief slideshow of random acts ensues before he or she snaps out of it. That was me. And all I envisioned was a bunch of ambulance-chasing lawyers. In just a year's time, what had once looked like a promising profession, turned into a trendy career that seemingly had room for everybody. So I left. I no longer wanted to be a lawyer or attend law school. But I had no idea what my next move was going to be. That was until the first day of official classes.

One of my first classes on that Monday was PG104: Introduction to Political Theory with Professor Arpad Kadarkay. He was an older Hungarian man with a thick accent and glasses. This was going to be my first official lesson in politics. Prior, I had no idea what politics was. I had no interest in any local or national elections. I cared little about Clinton's presidency or what was going on in the news. My earliest recollection of politics was the 1988 presidential election between George Bush and Mike Dukakis. I was in the first grade, and my teacher had decided to do a mock election in class in honor of election day for the president. She told the students nothing besides who the candidates were and told us to write a "B" for Bush or "D" for Dukakis, and afterward she would go around and collect all the slips. I am sure there was a lesson about democracy in there, and whoever received the most votes was going to win. Looking back, I wonder if my teacher knew what harm she was doing or if she even knew at all that presidents weren't elected democratically. I'm not even sure if I knew that by the time I reached Professor Kadarkay's class. What I do know is that I had written down a "D" for Dukakis. He lost the election in class that day, and he lost the election to George Bush later that day. The only other lesson I had received in politics and government was the "bill from Capitol Hill" commercials that used to play during Sesame Street and my other Saturday morning cartoons.

This class was unlike any other class that I had taken before. Not just in the course content, and it wasn't just the readings. It was how Professor Kadarkay taught it. He strutted around class slowly, pacing back and forth from side to side. He rarely sat down. The topics in the course covered themes of justice, equality, fairness, and political leadership. I remember flipping through the course syllabus as soon as we got it until I got to the books and the reading list for the semester. I was looking for Machiavelli's *The Prince*. It became a prominent book in the hip-hop community once 2Pac had read it in jail and changed his rap name to Makaveli on his last album while he was still alive. Until now, I had not been able to read it. To be honest, I did not know of a place to buy books, at least not history books that couldn't be found at the grocery store. I thought that if this book had made such an impact on his life, I had to read it. As soon as I found it, I closed the syllabus and fixated back on the professor making his way around the room, asking students to introduce themselves. As the class went on, he continued to strut around the class, occasionally chewing on the ends of his glasses before pointing them at a student and asking them to speak. He rarely asked questions and waited for students to answer. He just pointed at them with his glasses and expected them to talk about the topic at hand or just what they were thinking. I remember thinking to myself, this may be the first time that I recall a teacher actually caring to ask a student what they thought. I was used to getting taught at not really having a back and forth. He allowed us and gave us the opportunity to say whatever we were thinking, right or wrong, but he would ask us to defend ourselves or at least justify our thought in some way. I left that class on the first day thinking: I got it. I can do that!

By the first week of classes, I knew just what I wanted to do, although I was not sure how to get there. I wanted to champion Black political causes. Maybe I would run for office someday. I could actually see myself as an elected official someday! Perhaps I would go back to my hometown and run for mayor. It was a great idea. I would use my time in Puget Sound to learn as much about the political process as I could, especially how it impacted Black people. I'm not sure if I could have gotten a better crash course in politics than my time spent at the University of Puget Sound. Not just in the classroom, but as I learned and contemplated the realities of my existence, there was no better place to generate my own political identity and what would later become my own personal philosophy. The University of Puget Sound was located on the north side of town in Tacoma, Washington. As you drive into or away from campus in generally all directions, you can see the segregation evolve as the streets and homes get more dilapidated the further you move away from campus. Nearby was "hilltop," a predominately Black area that was known for crime and gang activity. Everywhere else consisted of a scattering of poor, middle-class whites. The university itself was about 2 percent Black/African American and over 80 percent white. But the university was not just predominantly white; its student body was an upper-class white that I had yet to encounter back home. Sure, Portland was segregated, but we had decided earlier on in our youth that we wanted nothing to do with crossing the Willamette River to the west side of town. The wealthier and whiter side of Portland had been known to be hostile to Black people, and the last thing we ever wanted was to be stuck over there. There was class inequality on the east side, but it was mainly between poor and middle-class whites. Those of us who lived below "snob hill" had a sense of unity and almost a badge of courage from living below the hill, and most considered us to be the toughest ones of the bunch. Being Black and lower middle-class, my mother worked two jobs and sacrificed many days away from home to make sure we weren't poor, which came with no particular advantage. Northeast Portland was considered the "ghetto" part of town that whites feared due to its reputation for crime and gang activity. It just so happened to also be primarily Black. I grew up with family that lived in the area, and it was still known as the place to get culturally relevant food and clothing, so it was nothing for me to visit the area. Hilltop Tacoma felt like northeast Portland to me, and by my sophomore year in college, I was living there.

At Puget Sound, I was confronted with what I would call extreme class and income inequality. The self-titled "Harvard of the Northwest" had attracted some of the offspring from nearby Nintendo and Microsoft that had executive campuses nearby, and they were about to give me a crash course in politics and economics, unlike anything I had experienced previously. Pulling into the parking lot in my 1984 Volkswagen Rabbit that I had hustled to buy, I was astonished by how many Mercedes and Lexus cars were in the student lot. My roommate was your stereotypical privileged white boy from Arizona, with pictures of his high school sweetheart back home on his desk, just a year younger, and his CD case with a sprinkling of rap music. During every semester break, I went home to friends and family in Portland; the majority of students returned to campus from Mt Bachelor with tans from Lake Shasta or pictures from studying abroad. I had gotten a credit card that I had maxed out the first semester buying books. Nobody had told me that you had to buy books in college! My puny $500 limit would not last very long, with $120 biology books and the five other books that were required for just one class. I had to closely monitor the expenses on my prepaid food plan, which left me few opportunities to take advantage of the basement cellar that consisted of pizza, breadsticks, and ice cream. This was my first dose of what I was told was "real life." We were all adults on that campus without any parents, free to move and make decisions on our own, and yet I was still at a disadvantage. And this made me angry.

The politics of socialization and witnessing the contradictory nature of the student body made UPS a horrible place for self-discovery around racial identity. University students, staff, and faculty had proclaimed themselves to be so open-minded and champions of diversity, despite their pathetic enrollment numbers of Black students. Every club or social institution had its "token" Black person that it paraded around as an expression of open-mindedness. I was "more" Black at Puget Sound than I had previously been in high school, but it made little difference when you only see roughly five percent of the entire student body in between the dining hall and schedule of classes. As a result, I clung to my Blackness even tighter and more defiantly; more tattoos, cornrows, bigger chains, and more explicit gangsta rap.

Perhaps no event affected me more than the annual "drummers for peace" event that took place on campus. The purpose of the drummers for peace platform was to embody a message of peace in favor of humanity and to engage the concepts of freedom and justice through drumming. At Puget Sound, this consisted of upper-class whites, some in dreadlocks, pretending to be poor, drumming up in the trees in between dorms for 24 hours. After that, they climbed down, hopped in their cars, and continued on with their lives as if any tangible change had been made. There was no association with racial injustice, or any definable measurement of progress based on what they were doing. The lesson I learned about the white liberal is that these phony practices of radicalism made them feel better. Nothing more, nothing less. And feeling better was good enough for them. They were not interested in actual change. They just wanted to feel better as participants in the oppression of others.

Keep in mind that up until this point, I had no little to no understanding of party politics and ideology. Left, right, Republican, Democrat, all were of no consequence to me, and I did not identify with any of them. I had yet to develop my party ideology. What I did know was that I was against racists and racism and anyone who benefited from or espoused racist views or associated with racist people. The other thing I knew for certain was that there was extreme income inequality in

America, and I hadn't noticed anyone caring or talking about it. But I was witnessing it with my own eyes while at the same time experiencing it in my own life. Thus, the two issues that concerned me the most were race and class. The University of Puget Sound, like my hometown of Portland, Oregon, was failing in both of these areas.

Both places had reputations for being beacons of open-mindedness and progressive liberal thinking. They were considered branches of what would be identified by the hippie generation of the 1960s and 1970s that was supposedly more open and understanding to the plight of Black people. They were far from the racist, confederate flag-loving conservative that was supposed to symbolize closed-mindedness. If Black people were going to find an ally in anyone outside of our own community, the white liberal was supposedly the closest thing to it. Unfortunately, my growing up in Portland had prepared me all too well for the white liberal in America. They never used the n-word and coached Black kids on their sports teams, but they still didn't want Blacks dating their children and definitely would not go out of their way to sacrifice their privilege for the development of Black people. Their brand of liberalism and progressive thinking stopped at the advancement of the material conditions of African Americans. They preferred the subjective, non-tangible, universal good feelings of such things as justice, equality, and freedom. All concepts that meant something different to everyone and were damn near impossible to achieve. These were things that white people could strive for openly without any racial conflict while at the same time appearing to be allies for Black people, but when these subjective terms never came to fruition, they could blame anyone but themselves even though they had done very little.

There was nothing in national politics that moved me, so I was a political blank slate. But my experiences in Portland and at Puget Sound had made me resent Democrats. During the first summer break from college, I went home to Portland and had cable TV once again and watched nothing but the *Bill O'Reilly Show* on the Fox News channel nightly. I occasionally caught Hannity and Colmes for the back and forth, but the way Mr O'Reilly used to rail on Democrats was quite impressive. I remember having dinner with my mom when he was on and her saying, "the man is full of shit, but he makes some great points." With no political background or party affiliation, I was free to create and develop my own political identity and beliefs. And I rejected liberalism.

There was little consolation for me in the curriculum of either Politics and Government or African American Studies at the university. The minor in African American studies consisted of only one class that centered on the Black experience: African American Studies 101. Other courses that could be taken to satisfy the minor in African American studies consisted of ones devoted to jazz, poetry, and social inequalities, all held in departments outside of the African American Studies department, and none of them were, what would be called, Afrocentric or centering the Black/African experiences in the study of the theme being explored in class. Of course, the one course that did was also the only class offered by the one Black professor at the university. I studied rigorously and treated the subject matter delicately since I knew from my early childhood days of watching slavery and civil rights movement videos, when at their conclusion and it's time for analysis, all the kids would turn around or stare into the abyss in silence, waiting for the one Black student in class to explain how Black people felt and to offer an opinion first before anyone else feels comfortable, that person was going to be me. But unlike in high school, I was more prepared and committed to teaching them a lesson every chance I got.

The Politics and Government curriculum was no better. Outside of political theory, I had very little interest in much the professors were teaching outside of American government, which I felt was essential to my potential as a future elected official. Courses in comparative politics and international relations struck no chord with me. I did not see how studying the regimes in China or Germany was going to benefit me, or Black people at all, for that matter, especially after what I prioritized as more immediate domestic needs and concerns. As part of the liberal arts education, I also had to take required courses in math and the hard sciences. I saw these classes as "need to pass" only since I had firmly staked my claim in politics and government. But I knew what I liked and wanted to study. My disdain for political science, or perhaps the way it was being taught and conceptualized, eventually led me to the field of philosophy. Every chance I had to take a class in philosophy, I took it. It was very closely related to what would be my specialty: political theory.

Political theory involves the study of the history of political thought as well as problems in contemporary political life that have a philosophical dimension. Thus, there was a lot of crossover in themes and concepts and, in some cases, readings between political theory and philosophy. At one point, I considered switching my major to philosophy. I could envision myself as a

Black Socrates wandering around town, aimlessly questioning the meaning of life and the political behavior of people. It was until I was told "you'll never get a job with a major in philosophy," that I reconsidered philosophy and stuck with political science. I could essentially continue to do political philosophy, which was good enough for me and would allow me to be "employable" under the banner of political science, although much more of what I did, and was interested in, was philosophizing. After taking the core requirements in political science, I was left to explore my passion for philosophy through electives and would spend the next two years crafting and exploring the field until I graduated.

Philosophy taught me invaluable lessons and skills that would set the foundation for everything I would become as a student. First, a love of learning and the importance of intellectual virtue in being smart for its own sake. And second, the requirement of questioning everything, because everything is questionable. Before I even got too deep into the readings, I was enthralled with the practice of philosophy. Thinking. Contemplating. Questioning everything, including the meaning of life and my own existence. Until that point, I had never had the opportunity to question anything. I had always, for the most part, done what my mother had told me. We come from a primarily Christian background that supports a hierarchal way of life and one's commitment to the church. Some of my earliest days consisted of Sunday school and sitting in the front row at the church where my uncle was the pastor. What and who was good and bad had already been determined and left without much room for questioning. Philosophy made me a new student and a new type of student. A new student in that I had completely reorganized and rearranged my academic pursuits. A new type of student in that I was going to start completely over in what I believed in and how I approached life in college and out of it. The tools I learned in philosophy continue to frame not only my personal life but particularly my academic career and intellectual life. Life was 90 percent mental. Time to go to work.

# Making education my own: an intellectual foundation

Navigating my subsequent years as a student, I knew one thing: I needed an intellectual mentor, and to be great I had to set out on my own course and create my own lane. Those whom I perceived to be the great thinkers I read about and watched in documentaries had either one or usually both of these things. I had neither, but it wouldn't take long for me to find them. What I needed was an identity. A well-crafted identity that I could believe to the point where I was willing to accept the fate of Socrates, who would rather accept death than betray what he believed and knew to be true. I already had a blueprint of expectations: I was going to be the academic Tupac Shakur. But like his skills on the mic, I had yet to produce such skills via the classroom. The courses I took would help provide me with the tools I needed to create and develop what would become my own identity and personal political philosophy. Both of my needs, a person or idea to guide me and a lane of my own, both came from the same source: me. Descartes argued one of the most basic tenets of philosophy: "I think, therefore I am." The point was that my own existence and potential as a human being started with an "I." Without the existence of a me, I couldn't accomplish or do anything, let alone accomplish anything great. Thus, the condition of the "I," that is, me, was going to be the first thing that I had to train and condition.

Nothing else mattered until I had full and complete mastery of myself and my most intimate fears, beliefs, and insecurities. I was going to have to dive deep and confront all these things and demonstrate a level of mastery that would allow me to overcome my own self. Ninety percent of life is mental. Who do I spend most of my time with? What stopped or enabled me to meet or exceed my own standards? The answer was always me. Know thyself first and foremost. I was useless and could not help my family or anyone else if I was not the best version of myself that I could be. Without full mastery and confidence in who Stephen was, Stephen could not do anything worthwhile for anyone. And in the process of doing for myself in pursuit of becoming the best version of myself, I could also help others. This meant I had to learn and overcome things that I did not like about myself. More importantly, I had to learn what I was capable of, how far I was willing to go, what I liked, and what I did not like. The only way I could step out into the world in full confidence, ready and willing to conquer whatever came my way, was through a deep understanding and mastery of myself as an individual. If I knew myself and everything that I was capable of, there would be nothing that anyone could do to me or words that could offend me, to throw me off my path, or cause me to go outside my own lane. I was going to master my lane; live and dwell in it so that nothing or no one could intrude upon it. At the same time, I was an adult, no longer living at home, in a new place where no one knew me personally and had no insights into my previous baggage and shortcomings. I was the freest I could ever be. I was free to completely reinvent myself and become whoever and whatever I wanted to be. This was an opportunity that was too good to pass up.

There are four main theorists or theories that provided the foundation for my political identity: Plato's Philosopher King, Machiavelli's Prince, Nietzsche's concept of will, and Marxism. None of these concepts or theories depended on or centered race or Blackness at all. None of the theorists were Black, and none of their proposed theories were racially specific or discussed the Black experience particularly. Most political thought begins with Plato's *Republic* and the dialogue of Socrates, and this would be my first introduction to reading political philosophy. As I understood politics, it was all about decision-making, particularly at the government level. To simplify it, I remember it as the "who, what, when, where, how, and why" of governing. The purpose of government is the common good. The common good refers to either what is shared and beneficial for all or most members of a given community or, alternatively, what is achieved by citizenship, collective action, and active participation in the realm of politics and public service. Despite its interpretations, most political thinkers agree that this is the end of government—the pursuit of what is good for all its citizens—and that "no government should become the perverted servant of special interests" (Diggs, 1973: 284). Conceiving of government in this way made sense to me as the only sensible way for any government to be legitimate. Thinking of a country or a community as a team and not just a collection of individuals gives credence to the concept of the common good. The purpose of government is to serve both "we" and "me." Playing sports, where there was always the awareness of there being no "I" in "team," helped this concept make perfect sense.

The first order of business in exploring the basics of politics was the "who." Who constitutes the government: one, few, or many. One political actor represents some form of monarchy or dictatorship; a few political actors represent an aristocracy or oligarchy, and where there are many political actors, we have democracy. Plato's philosopher king rests on the idea that the best form of government is that in which philosophers rule. The notion of the "philosopher king" is that the philosopher is the only person who can be trusted to rule well. According to Plato, philosophers are both morally and intellectually suited to rule: morally because it is in their nature to love truth and learning so much that they are free from the greed and lust that tempts others to abuse power; and intellectually because they alone can gain full knowledge of reality. In the allegory in Plato's *Republic*, Socrates describes a group of people who have lived chained to the wall of a cave all their lives, facing a blank wall. The people watch shadows projected on the wall from objects passing in front of a fire behind them and give names to these shadows. The shadows are the prisoners' reality but are not accurate representations of the real world. Socrates explains how the philosopher is like a prisoner who is freed from the cave and comes to understand that the shadows on the wall are actually not reality at all. A philosopher aims to understand and perceive the higher levels of reality. Plato then supposes that one prisoner is freed and escapes the cave. The freed prisoner would think that the world outside the cave was superior to the world he had experienced in the cave and would attempt to share this with the prisoners remaining in the cave. The prisoners, according to Plato, would infer from the returning man's blindness that the journey out of the cave had harmed him and that they should not undertake a similar journey. Plato concludes that the prisoners, if they were able, would therefore reach out and kill anyone who attempted to drag them out of the cave. This was not only an exercise in intellectualism, but a lesson in leadership as well.

Machiavelli's *Prince* became the personification of what I aimed to be and how I would structure my personal life. *The Prince* served as a practical guide for ruling and leadership. Machiavelli offers practical advice on a variety of matters, including the advantages and disadvantages that attend various routes to power, how to acquire and hold new states, how to deal with internal insurrection, how to make alliances, and how to maintain a strong military. Implicit in these chapters are Machiavelli's views regarding free will, human nature, and ethics. Machiavelli's underlying view is that lofty ideals translate into bad government. This premise is especially true with respect to personal virtue. Certain virtues may be admired for their own sake, but for a prince to act in accordance with virtue is often detrimental to the state. Similarly, certain vices may be frowned upon, but vicious actions are sometimes indispensable for the good of the state. Machiavelli combines this line of reasoning with another: that obtaining the goodwill of the populace is the best way to maintain power. Virtue, according to Machiavelli, aims to reduce the power of fortune over human affairs because fortune keeps men from relying on themselves. A prince who possesses the virtue of mastery can command fortune and manage people to a degree never before thought possible.

The greatest lesson I took away from Machiavelli's prince concerns the issue of the reputation of the leader. Although some measure of cruelty is necessary to maintain order, Machiavelli contends that a prince should be careful in his exercise of cruelty, tempering it with humanity and prudence. Machiavelli then asks whether being feared or loved is preferable. Ideally, a prince should be both loved and feared, but this state of affairs is difficult to attain. Forced to make a choice, it is much better to be feared than loved. This is because men, by nature, are "ungrateful, fickle, dissembling, anxious to flee danger, and covetous of gain." In times of remote danger, they are willing to take risks for their prince, but if the danger is real, they turn against their prince. It is easy to break a bond of love when the situation arises, but the fear of punishment is always effective, regardless of the situation. The lessons from Machiavelli's *Prince* continue to play a significant role in my personal and professional life.

Perhaps, no one contributed to my worldview as much as Friedrich Nietzsche. Nietzsche believed himself to be the harbinger of what he calls "great politics." He maintained that political liberalism's advocacy of human rights and political equality are a direct result of Christianity's push for equal human dignity in the "eyes of God." For Nietzsche, this ideology presents a form of decadence or bad faith that humans no longer need to indulge in. The "ideal love of humanity" has political implications because this defining characteristic of humanity must be identified in contrast with the passionate and subjective "will to power" and domination over others, which is the actual root of all human choices. According to Nietzsche, objective normative truths would not be able to provide a basis for political legitimacy in secular societies because the majority of people would have no means of recognizing it as such (Shaw, 2010: 9). Democratic political structures must necessarily foster a smallness of spirit in the cultural and social spheres because they rest upon the belief in human equality. The belief in human equality lacks an objective truth, and thus provides no basis for political legitimacy in secular, democratic societies.

What Nietzsche admires most in the social and political realm is the Napoleonic "hardness of hammer," the rejection of the unmanly and morbid pity in favor of "great ideas." The will to power describes what Nietzsche may have believed to be the main driving force in humans. It is best understood as an irrational force found in all individuals that can be channeled toward different ends. The will to power, as Nietzsche conceives of it, is neither good nor bad. It is a basic drive found in everyone, but one that expresses itself in many different ways. The strong, healthy, masterly types confidently impose their values on the world directly. The weak, by contrast, seek to impose their values in a more cunning, roundabout way by making the strong feel guilty about their health, strength, egotism, and pride. One particular form of the will to power that Nietzsche devotes much attention to is what he calls "self-overcoming." Here the will to power is harnessed and directed toward self-mastery and self-transformation, guided by the principle that "your real self lies not deep within you but high above you."

Last, Marx conceived of labor as completing man's "species life" or human nature. According to Marx, labor is the natural and desirable activity of the human being. The role and purpose for which humans exist are inherently tied to labor. Labor presents the ability for individuals to transform the world, take nature as we see it, and change the material conditions in which we exist. For Marx, the estrangement of labor causes a feeling of isolation and separation between the individual and the outside community. The theoretical basis of alienation within the capitalist mode of production is that the worker invariably loses the ability to determine life and destiny when deprived of the right to think (conceive) of themselves as the director of their own actions; to determine the character of the said actions; to define relationships with other people; and to own those items of value from goods and services, produced by their own labor. Although the worker is an autonomous, self-realized human being, as an economic entity the worker is directed toward goals and diverted to activities that are dictated by the bourgeoisie— those who own the means of production—in order to extract from the worker the maximum amount of surplus value in the course of business competition among industrialists. Capitalism has distorted human relations to the point that they are not controlled by the participants themselves. This, in turn, leads to the separation of things that belong to each other naturally, which then results in antagonism between things that should be working together to achieve common goals and outcomes.

Within the capitalist mode of production, the individual loses their control over their work. They lose their ability to think, determine their destiny, define their relations with others, and own things of value. Ultimately workers lose the liberty to think for themselves and to make their own decisions since they have no control over their work. They do not own the goods that they produce, nor do they have the freedom to produce what they want. Thus, the individual becomes animal-like in their thought as they lose their ability to think. Their goals are directed toward activities that are owned and dictated by the bourgeoisie. The individual is alienated from the products that they manufacture because they do not own them. They are owned and disposed of by the bourgeoisie. Thus, he cannot own the things that he produces. He is paid minimum wages, and the returns of his labor are significantly low. This leads to exploitation of the worker. Workers do not have control over the process of production. The work conditions and organization are all determined by the bourgeoisie without taking the individual into consideration. The division of labor further aggravates this alienation. According to Marx, the ability to consciously shape things around us is what makes us human. However, capitalism takes away 'Gattungswesen' or the essence of being human. The individual's labor is forced and coerced. The kind of work that the individual is made to do has no correlation with his interests or passion. The wealth that is created by the worker is owned by the bourgeoisie who is driven by profit maximization. This leads to the strengthening of classes in society which hinders the individual's ability to determine his actions. Under capitalism, the worker is seen as an entity that can be used and traded to maximize production and profits. Workers are entrenched in the world of cutthroat competition to get the maximum wages possible from the bourgeoisie, who in turn try to get the maximum labor from the worker. This alienation also arises inevitably from the class structure and division of labor in capitalist society.

These four theories would become the theoretical framework for not only the rest of my academic career but also how I structured my life. As a student-athlete, I experienced the importance of teamwork. Plato's emphasis on the order of the individual, society, and of the three parts being in harmony resonated with me. I even started saying "everything in moderation" as a reminder and occasional excuse for experimentation. Like in football, everyone has a role in society to play. As a person who has been in a leadership role, and foresaw myself as a leader in the future, I paid close attention to studies in leadership. My first book would stem from my original notes and a theoretical framework from my undergraduate days. Plato's "allegory of the cave" also struck a chord with me that I had previously felt listening to 2Pac's music: be prepared to suffer and be betrayed. It was a risky business setting out on this philosophical landscape; people were not going to like you, and you should be prepared to be stabbed in the back by the very people you are trying to save. The story of Plato's philosopher king and allegory of the cave also fell in line with what I remembered from church: suffering was inescapable, but it can be overcome.

If Plato's philosopher king and allegory of the cave gave me a purpose to lead for the common good of my community and not my own self-interest, Machiavelli's *Prince* would provide me with the road map. Plato had taught me what leadership was: service. Machiavelli taught me how to lead—the day-to-day behaviors and responses that I would need to accomplish my goals. I bought and read everything by and about Machiavelli that I could get my hands on. Stanley Bing's *What Would Machiavelli Do?: The Ends Justify the Meanness* was a contemporary take on the *Prince* that offers day-to-day, practical applications of leadership that I frequently read.

The whole theme of the book took me back to that one-on-one conversation with my father before he left. Up until that moment, his proclamation that I was a king sounded more like an empowering last goodbye speech from a father to his son, than a passing of the torch. But a decade later, I had found myself in the position to need and rely on that message, especially the mentality it required, more than ever. Now, I was taking his words seriously. He was right. But I had no idea how to be a king. I was ill-prepared to lead anything great. My leadership was based on old-fashioned charisma and a sense of humor, but too many failures had left me looking for something else, something that would work. Something that would last.

Machiavelli made me a realist and eliminated any possibility of me keeping any ideological ties to liberalism. Too many people lived in a fantasy world, imagining and philosophizing about a world that should be instead of the world that actually existed. Those subjective, feel-good words like justice and equality were nothing but idealistic hopes. People moved and operated within the political atmosphere hoping and praying about an idealistic society and government that had never been and had very little chance of existing. This would be my main problem with democracy and American government as I continued my education. Liberals were unrealistic. Black people were unrealistic. Working-class, poor people were unrealistic. All living in a fantasy world in which if they just worked hard, were "good people," integrated with whites and were unthreatening that America could be a fair and just society. Whatever the hell that meant.

I was sure that a fair and just society meant different things to different people, especially to Black and white people in America. Black people were unrealistic in thinking that whites would ever treat them fairly or as equal participants in this democracy with them. Neither the founding fathers nor any white person that I had read about or come across had ever imagined a society where Blacks and whites in America were equals. More so, the strategy that was being employed by Black people in America was idealistic and unrealistic as well. Did Blacks actually believe that whites would magically have a change of heart and completely restructure not only their minds and feelings, but the institutional racism that perpetuated Black oppression in order to dismantle that same system that had made them first-class citizens with dominion over Blacks for over 400 years?

I had the same problem with working-class and poor people. Did they actually believe that rich people with power were just going to hand over and redistribute the wealth to eliminate the gross and ever-growing income inequality in this country? Like they were going to just wake up one day and say to themselves, "I've earned enough. Maybe we have been taking advantage of poor people. Let's give some back." Get real! This idealistic, kumbaya, multicultural society that people kept talking about under the guise of liberalism and progressivism was completely unrealistic. Power is never going to be exchanged between white and Black or rich and poor peacefully. And sitting by and asking nicely, waiting for your oppressor to undergo an emotional transformation that triggers a change of heart, was a terrible strategy. People of this ilk are delusional.

But Machiavelli's lesson worked not just in the classroom, but as a personal road map as well. Until then, my Christian framework of morality had remained intact. It was now under massive attack. Philosophy had taught me to question everything. Machiavelli taught me to question morality. All the traditional virtues of being well-behaved, honest, getting along with people, being a nice guy, and forgiveness—all had to be reinvestigated and questioned. What it meant to be "happy," "angry," and "nice" was irrelevant and I threw them all out the window under the wide umbrella of subjectivity, meaning they had no real, absolute meaning. They meant something different to everyone. I knew 95-pound homeless crackheads who would be considered "happy," so what was the purpose of people "just wanting to be happy?" That seemed like too low a bar. I had tried to exhibit all of the "good virtues" of traditional Christian morality throughout my life: fit in, be nice to people, turn the other cheek and forgive, and practice honesty and kindness to others. Been there, done that. And where had it gotten me? Nowhere. I was still a poor, young Black male with no power, little influence, and no valuable reputation, simply a JAG (just another guy). If anything, trying to be some nice, forgiving guy who was friends with everyone had done me more harm than good. These concepts no longer held space in my mind as personal attributes that I should hope to attain or strive for. I would, instead, reinvent and reclassify all these concepts and tailor them to my personal aspirations where they could be most useful.

I remember an example that Professor Kadarkay had given in class while discussing Plato's theory of justice and what it meant. To this day, I still use this demonstration in class to question my students' beliefs about justice and fairness. He asked how many of us had told someone who was not a family member that they loved them. About 90 percent, if not all, of the students raised their hands. He then asked, now, how many of you hate or would never talk to that person again? Mostly while laughing, the overwhelming majority of those students all put their hands back up. Assuming for a second that we as students, or anyone for that matter, actually knows what love is, all of us had once had those feelings for someone that we now did not like at all. Whatever attachment or emotional connection love could bring could also very easily vanish into something much worse than indifference but full-blown disdain. Then what, he responded, is the value of treating someone you love differently from anyone else if that love is only fickle and temporary at best? He got me. The abandonment of close friends and the lost relationships had left me more cynical and in a worse spiritual and emotional state than if I had been left alone and rarely interacted with anyone. This taught me an invaluable lesson that would aid me throughout the rest of my career: ideas over people. People were, in fact, fickle, ignorant animals, no better or worse than any other creature of God's creation. If I was going to survive, I had to acknowledge the reality of the human condition and not be idealistic and delusional in thinking that being nice and loving people was going to be all I needed. People died and were mortal, but ideas could live forever. People could let you down or have character flaws that embarrass not only them but also their fans or followers. There was always a "what about-ism" when you mention the name of an idol who has some mistake or flaw in their character. In order to make it, I had to shed any long-lasting affinity for any particular individual, instead appreciating their ideas or accomplishments. My favorite musician as a child was Michael Jackson. I grew up singing Jackson 5 songs in the bathtub and watching every video he ever made. It would later come out that he was accused of misbehavior with regard to inviting young boys to sleep in his bed with him, which led many to abandon him and his incredible playlist. The same thing happened to Tupac Shakur over his reputation as a violent thug. Whenever each artist ever came up, I would retreat to my stance of "terrible person, greatest artist of all time." "Well, what about what he did in …?" People are terrible creatures. I have no faith in any of them. I believe in ideas over people.

If the goal was to "do the least amount harm," it was best to start with the "I" who exists as Descartes had suggested. I decided to abandon the traditional Christian framework of morality in favor of something that was more realistic and practical for my day-to-day existence: whatever works. Great people were going to be remembered forever. Whether they were good people or not did not matter, and yet everyone was entirely focused on being a good person or at least having a public image as such. Was Walt Disney a good person? How about Thomas Jefferson? Both of these men were in the history books, would be remembered forever with lasting legacies, and were considered to be great men. Both were racist and, by any measure of Judeo-Christian moral values, were absolutely terrible people. But none of those things seemed to matter. But why? Because of what they had accomplished. Their accomplishments, doing great deeds, outweighed and surpassed any notions of being a good person. What you actually did with your life mattered much more than how you behaved or made people feel. Treating people "right" and having a lot of friends meant absolutely nothing without a great accomplishment to accompany it. And if being a "good" person and treating people right was going to be a barrier to accomplishing great things, then I was more than ready to get rid of these traits. What I needed more than anything was to be smart, innovative, flexible, courageous, and strong-willed. With these tools, I could accomplish anything.

Left without a moral framework, yet still unable to completely abandon the notion of faith, Nietzsche's Übermensch was the perfect replacement. He taught me that I could develop my own better set of morals than those practiced by general society. My personal, better set of morals would be my justification for the "whatever it takes" orthodoxy that I was now practicing. The Übermensch represents a shift from otherworldly Christian values and manifests the grounded human ideal. Nietzsche's declaration that "God was dead" and that we humans were responsible for his death which resulted in a world of poor, subjective morality was real. I read about the white Christians of the South who routinely beat, murdered, and raped Black people, all while clutching their bibles with a firm belief that they were destined for heaven. Really!? What God and what Christianity would allow for such blatant hypocrisy? Any faith that allowed, enabled, or perpetuated such a low and pathetic standard of morals should be rejected wholeheartedly. Those were the morals of the masses; certainly, no one of extraordinary intelligence or standing could be expected to meet such a low standard. Consequently, those of extraordinary skill and intelligence were to operate from a separate, better set of morals. Being "nice," "forgiving," "slow to anger," and turning the other cheek was for the weak and weak-willed. They needed this low set of standards because they cared too much about worldly possessions and reputation rather than accomplishing anything great. I refused to be judged by the expectations and standards of the majority of society. I had known and encountered people who were "successful," wealthy, popular, and had good grades or jobs, but 99 percent of those people were white, middle-upper-class people who had either one or a combination of advantages: a network from their close friends or parents, money from their parents or grandparents, or who had just gotten by through no particular skill or talent other than being nice and making friends with everyone. They had not demonstrated any exceptional talent or skill to get where they were. I was not impressed by their status. I was poor and Black with no connections and no reputation of any benefit. What I had accomplished was much more impressive than anything they had done. I was a nobody. They all had head starts. I had nothing. They had wealthy parents and connections, and white privilege. We were not the same, and the comparisons started to become offensive. If I was going to do great things, I could not live by the same pathetic standards as everyone else. I had to set out and do my own thing, guided by my own set of beliefs and principles. A higher calling demanded higher standards.

There was also an aura of responsibility and accountability that I was deeply attracted to. An element of individual expression and demonstration of the strength of one's individual will was a failure to blame others and accepting full responsibility for success or failure with no excuses. This also paralleled my experiences in sports. Win or lose, nobody really cared who was hurt or who didn't play. It was very zero-sum. But being part of a team allowed for the sharing of blame or credit that always enabled the individual winner or loser a certain amount of coverage or protection from either being too celebrated or receiving too much blame. An individual player could only accomplish so much without the help and assistance of teammates and coaches. In life, these circumstances did not entirely exist. I was going to either succeed or fail based on my own doing. If I was a failure, no one was going to care that I was poor, or Black, or didn't have many friends. I did not accomplish what I set out to, and that was going to be it. Too many people were comfortable in their failure because it had become a widely accepted practice to blame your individual shortcomings on your parents, or on being poor, or if I only had a chance to play, I could have made it, type of mentality. By the same token, people who had made it and became successful always had to share the credit with their parents and give thanks to friends and family, and I "couldn't have done it without"-isms that I wanted to avoid. The biggest reward was in establishing my own lane and lifestyle that fostered success. But it also came with the biggest risk: I was going to either receive all the credit or I was going to receive all the blame. Not being able to point to someone else and say, "I couldn't have done it without you," is the greatest accomplishment an individual can attain. When people asked, "how'd you make it?" it would be easy to respond with, "nothing but my own sheer will and determination." The problem was that, on the other hand, if I failed in setting my own path and doing things my own way, then when I was approached with the same question but in reverse, "why didn't you succeed?" my only response could be due to my own failures and shortcomings. I was not going to be able to point the finger at someone else or some institution and say, "because of them!" It was my choice to set out on my own and not heed the advice of others. I made the decisions; thus, I was going to get and deserve all the blame. Conversely, and more importantly, if I succeeded, I was going to get all the credit. No one else was going to be responsible for my success other than me. And this was the greatest achievement that an individual can accomplish. Either I was going to get all the credit or all the blame. That was the risk. I was determined to risk everything that I had and bet on what I knew I could count on the most: me. With this piece, I was now set with all the personal tools and ideas that I needed to move forward academically.

# Exploring personal growth

My life was much more than academics, however. There was still navigating my personal life and interactions with other people that I had to master. Although these ideas would also structure my personal life, I had still not acquired a proper understanding of exercising these virtues in the reality of socialization. My previous educational experience was hampered by my high intelligence but diminished by my inability to associate and attach any social value to intellectualism. What good was being smart if I couldn't use it outside of the classroom in my day-to-day interactions with people? My love of philosophy had opened me to the notion of intellectual virtue and being smart for the sake of being smart, but I was yet to understand and see real-world examples of its value in my day-to-day.

That was until I met the person who would become my best friend in college. Aaron was also from Oregon but from the smaller town of Eugene, about 100 miles south of Portland and the hometown of the University of Oregon. Outside of my roommate and the people on the floor of my dorm, he was the first person I met at the first football meeting before classes had even started. He was a quarterback, and I was a running back, and it didn't take long before we came to the conclusion that we shared many mutual interests, including that we were both Politics and Government majors, but he had decided to go the pre-law route that I had already discarded. We took as many classes as we could together, and he took me to my first University of Oregon Ducks football game while visiting his mother in Eugene. He had come to Portland many times and met my family, and even took me to Palm Springs to meet his grandfather. Aaron certainly came from a place of privilege, but if you met him and interacted with him, you certainly wouldn't know it. A typical six-foot, average build guy with no fancy clothes or attention-grabbing jewelry or glasses or anything. He looked like just a guy, and for four years, we traveled up and down Interstate 5 in his faded navy blue Nissan Pathfinder that had more miles on it than my Volkswagen.

Until then, I had never been close friends with someone who exercised a similar intellectual veracity. Most of my friends were jocks my entire life. When we weren't in class, he would listen to all my crazy theories I was pulling from the course material but never shared when I was called on. I remember him always asking me, "why didn't you say that shit in class?" Together we fed off and encouraged each other's elitism, reinforcing a separate and higher form of being between ourselves by always referring to everyone else as "those people" and "these people." Constantly pushing the limits and taking unnecessary risks, only to shrug them off and laugh about them later as if we deserved to get away with it. In the big scheme of things, we were nobodies, but we had actually figured out how to live in such a way as to reinforce the feeling that we were better than other people. Not in physical strength or ability, money, looks, or popularity. But primarily, if for no other reason than because we believed it. That's it. And because of that, the confidence in my ideas and intellectual ability grew and strengthened.

As much as I appreciated having a partner in crime and ally on my intellectual journey, nothing was more beneficial than witnessing how Aaron used his intellect socially, even at times to my detriment. On a day-to-day basis, I watched him routinely outsmart other people, sometimes to get ahead or for personal gain, or other times for no other reason than the sport of it. As I was watching, I was learning the social value of intellect and intellectual virtue. Aaron was able to maneuver and manipulate entire situations with nothing more than word choice, body language, gentle syntax, and the reframing of context. There was no conversation too uncomfortable or controversial that he was not somehow able to escape unscathed. I watched in amazement at how he was able to verbalize belittling insults at people that would leave them saying thank you. As his friend, you would occasionally be victim of his free dealing ways, and yet when confronted, he had the blank shrug that said, "hey, it's just who I am, you know me," that paralyzed and halted any ill will. A group of us could literally sit down over lunch and reminisce and share notes about all the different times and ways that we had been left behind or stranded by him at a party or event, and yet nobody ever held any significant amount of disdain. He was not physically intimidating by any stretch of the imagination, and nobody would surely consider him to be any type of threat. There was not a room that he could not walk into that he would not figure out a way to integrate himself into. If the topic of conversation was controversial, he could formulate something memorable and thought-provoking without having taken any stance at all and without having offended anyone, all while getting his point across. One minute he could be in one room reciting the most offensive and degrading rap lyrics, while in the next, he could be in an entirely different crowd, playing the guitar and singing folk songs that he and his friends had written. Yet, at no point would anyone ever accuse him of being disingenuous, even when he was. Any significant criticism of social consequence just seemed to bounce right off him. I had never witnessed such a thing before, and it was an invaluable lesson.

## Conclusion

Now I know what people mean when they say that people come into your life for a reason or a season. During my most formative intellectual years, when I was consistently engaging and being in conflict with the courses and readings, working and massaging my own personal beliefs and identity, I was getting a lesson in intellectual practicality. Being smart was just as valuable inside the classroom as outside of the classroom. I could use my intellect, in the same way, to get things out of my personal life, as I similarly used it to get good grades. It consisted of learning and studying people and situations in addition to knowing exactly what was the most desirable and what to avoid in any given situation, and then how to position myself in order to properly navigate the space. I was used to being a student in the classroom and shedding the lessons and my intellectual cap for something much more "cool" and socially acceptable. I was ready to learn any and everything, if for no other reason than I could save it in my vault for nothing more than meaningless conversation or random trivia to deescalate an otherwise potentially hostile situation. Becoming a student outside the classroom as well as inside the classroom was going to be just as important to develop as my ability to support a thesis statement in an essay. Every conversation and interaction, no matter where it took place, was not only an opportunity to learn something but also an opportunity to demonstrate what I had learned. The world was a laboratory which I could use to conduct my own philosophical and social experiments. All the ideas and theories I pulled from different readings in the creation and development of my own intellectual Frankenstein could be tried out on friends, colleagues, and unsuspecting strangers. When it was time to graduate, Aaron and I went our separate ways, our careers and lives took us on separate paths. But the lesson that I needed to learn through this friendship made me enjoy the process of being a student while, at the same time, making me a better one.

# 2
# Graduate school adventures

By the time I graduated from UPS and was ready to attend graduate school, there were no longer any doubts about my future plans. I needed to get my PhD so I could become a university professor. Again, I was caught in the dilemma between doing what I was passionate about and doing what was going to be profitable and easier to find employment doing. Once again, political science had won out. After two years outside of academics, I couldn't wait to get back in the classroom and continue the journey, yet unlike in high school, I had already done pretty well as an undergraduate, and there wasn't going to be a need for a last-minute push to get straight As to muster up a respectable GPA. There was only one school on my list: the University of Nevada-Reno. It was no academic juggernaut, and I had never been to Nevada for a day in my life. I had only spent a total of three days in Reno while visiting my girlfriend at the time, who was spending her summer there working for her aunt in real estate. When the idea was brought up to move there together after graduation, I really didn't see the point in applying anywhere else. That would be the last time in my life I would ever consider anyone else but myself when making a career decision.

The graduate school lessons began for me before classes even started. The first lesson regarded my relationship with faith. In my intellectual pursuits and the quest to develop my own political identity, I had completely neglected church, much to the dismay of my mother, who would routinely check in with me and ask if I'd been "consulting the word." But the year prior to graduate school, I had spent working tedious jobs at a bowling alley, night auditor at a hotel, and customer service at Circuit City. I put on 60 pounds and looked and felt terrible. I was just roaming around in intellectual purgatory. It was time for me to leave Tacoma for good. As I was packing up from the room I was renting at the time, my good friend and former next-door neighbor, Mr Harper, called and told me to stop by and have some dinner with him before I left town. Since we used to have barbecue cook-offs when we lived next door to each other, I knew he was about to "put something on the grill," and after packing up all by myself, I could use some food and good conversation. The night started out as usual, joking about our barbecue recipes and hiding trash bags under the mattress, but as dinner finished up, his wife excused herself, and before you knew it, it was just the two of us sitting at the table. It was clear that Mr Harper could see that I was not doing well. The next words he says to me were, "are you ready to change your life?" Astonished but certainly not offended given the circumstances I was in, I said "yes" with very little hesitation. I needed all the help I could get! He got up from the table and left the room. I had no idea where he had gone or what he had in mind. He came back a few minutes later with a Bible in his hand that he said used to belong to his mother before she gave it to him. Then he asked if I was ready to be saved. I thought to myself, saved from what? He clearly meant rededicating myself and practicing my faith once again. At this point, I had nothing to lose, and something within me said to go along. Mr Harper wrote out a scripture from the Bible before giving it to me and told me to put it somewhere I would see it every day and to meditate on it for seven days. It was Romans 12:2, and I decided to put it in the visor in my car so that I would see it every time I pulled down the visor. From then until I left for Nevada, I completed a newly saved course and attended Bible Studies, men's group, and church every Sunday.

In my first test of faith, it only made sense that I would pray for the thing I wanted the most at the time, and that was to get into graduate school. It never crossed my mind to apply directly to the PhD programs. I had not been advised on the process but knew that getting a master's degree was the first step to getting my PhD in political science. I assumed that after my two years I would inevitably apply and complete the PhD program while at Nevada due to my familiarity with the majority of the doctoral courses transferring into the new program since they were taken at the same institution and therefore presumably would be similar to those for the master's. When it came time to apply to the University of Nevada, I was desperate due to the fact that my new intellectual persona had burned every bridge in Tacoma and Portland on the way out. My mother was about to get remarried and having her grown son living with her and her new husband in the early stages of a new marriage was not an option. Before getting in the car on the day I submitted my application materials, I decided to get down on my knees and pray. It had been a while, but I could literally think of no better time to test out my newly found faith. After attending such an expensive liberal arts school as an undergrad and knowing that going back to my mother for help was not an option, my biggest fear was not being able to afford graduate school. I knew I had a really good chance at getting in. I had done my research and provided a list of professors whom I wanted to work with and how I saw myself fitting into the program. But once again, I was dead poor. So, getting in alone was not going to be enough. Any financial assistance that was available to keep me from having to come out of pocket was going to be essential. So when I closed my eyes and hit my knees on that day, I said, "Lord, please get me into this graduate school. I don't even care how it's paid for as long as I get in, and I promise that if you get me in, I will go no matter what."

It wasn't long before I received my response in the mail confirming my acceptance into the program. I did not receive any teaching or research fellowships that would not only have paid my tuition but also provided a monthly stipend as pay for my working in the department as a grader/researcher for one of the professors, or for teaching a breakout lecture of one of the larger western civilization classes. Since I had received neither, all of my tuition was going to be paid through student loans, which I, of course, accepted. It became clear to me once I signed and returned the acceptance that I had just learned an invaluable lesson moving forward: if you decide to pray, be specific. It dawned on me that I had literally received everything that I had prayed for a few months earlier. I had gotten into graduate school, and it was paid for, but that was exactly it: there was no job, and no housing, just the cost of my tuition. I was going to be able to go to class, but I would be on my own for the rest. Be specific when you pray! That was an important lesson for a new graduate student to learn.

# Graduate school days: paying the price

When I first got to Nevada in June, I took the sunrise shift at UPS, which ran from 3 a.m. to 9 a.m., on an assembly line sorting packages six hours a day with my headphones in, taking package after package off trucks. This was the meaningless labor that Marx had warned us about in 1844! But I had no other choice if I was going to afford the small apartment I had rented a little south of campus, and those hours would not affect my class schedule since graduate courses were generally in the afternoon one day a week. Getting up at 3 a.m. to sort packages only lasted a month when my car broke down, leaving me no way to get across town to the facility. Since those jobs were easily refillable, after missing a day or two, I was out. With no car and no job, I had no other choice than to pack up whatever I could from my apartment and leave. With nowhere to go, I ended up in central Nevada in a tiny town called Yerington, wandering around the desert. There was a city library that had a computer with internet where you could sign up for the daily allotted 30 minutes maximum internet time. Without any phone service in that area, these 30 minutes were important for emailing my mom, which I did almost daily. The rest of my time was spent listening to my headphones and wandering around the desert in the dead of summer in a place I had never been.

Thirty days of wandering the Nevada desert came to an end a month later. It was now August, and classes would be starting soon. I still did not have a place to live and no way of paying for one. My mother was preparing to get married and had arranged for me to fly home to be at the wedding. When I got there, I was given a minivan that my stepdad had owned, but now that they had moved into a place together and consolidated their possessions, there was no longer any room for it, and it was taking up a parking space. He told me that we could take the back seat out of it, and I could have it if I wanted it. Having no other choice, of course, I took it. A good friend had an extra queen-size mattress from a previous move that he said I could have, which I also took, figuring I could sleep on it after I got the seats out. After picking it up and tying it to the roof, Friday morning, I was hitting the road back to Nevada to start classes on Monday in a minivan. Where I was going to go when I got there, I had not figured out yet. In the back of that van were all my possessions: a large duffle bag full of clothes and boxes with all the books that I had kept as an undergraduate student.

Before I could even get out of the Portland city limits, the mattress that I had clearly not secured down to the top of the van very well began to noticeably shift and slide from side to side. It was 4 a.m., and I had an eight-hour drive back to Reno. When the mattress flew off the back of the van while I was on Interstate 5, I did not think more than a second about turning around and going back for it. I was most fortunate that there was nobody directly behind me, or anyone else on the road for that matter, as to cause an accident or be waved down about the mattress I was leaving on the freeway.

When I finally got to Nevada, there were only two places that I could think of where I would be able to park relatively unnoticed and for free: a casino or a truck stop. With all that money circulating around casinos, the safest option was going to be a truck stop where my old, beaten-down van would fit right in with the other cars spread out among the parking spots. There was also going to be a free bathroom and fountain to refill my cup for next to nothing. The first night I pulled into that parking spot, turned the car off and climbed into the back of that van surrounded by books and clothes; I could not believe what I had signed up for. It was damn near impossible to sleep, and I had no idea what to expect. The next day was Sunday before the first day of classes as a graduate student. I had pulled in the night before, and with no idea where I was or in what part of town I was in, I decided to get up and walk around for the day. Little did I know that it was the last day of the rib cook-off! Often referred to as the Super Bowl of rib competitions on the national BBQ competition circuit, the annual Labor Day Weekend event spans more than six city blocks in the heart of downtown Sparks, Nevada. The streets were absolutely packed with people, and there was nothing but the smell of barbecue filling the air. For this event, two dozen of the country's best BBQ teams compete for nearly $20,000 in prize money, plus prestigious bragging rights. I was starving and had no money, and I had found myself in the middle of a barbecue cook-off festival! For hours I wandered through the streets of downtown Sparks, watching as people lined up for the best barbecue and assortment of side dishes in the country on that particular day. I went from station to station, hoping that someone would be dishing out samples at least. There were none.

To give myself some reprieve from the smells and the excruciating heat of Nevada summers, I decided to go into the nearby casino and watch football in the air-conditioned sportsbook. Anyone who was not outside getting barbecue was inside this casino gambling. After I found a small corner to charge my phone while I utilized the opportunity to watch all the football games for free, I realized that being inside with a room full of gamblers was no better than being outside with a street full of hungry people. In both situations, I was torturing myself by confronting my dire circumstances. Outside, people were eating in my face. Inside, people were seemingly blowing money in my face. At various times I slipped into an alternate trance-like state similar to sitcom television, where the star of the show stares blankly into the camera while the camera cuts to a variety of played-out situations before focusing back on the actor. That was me, but the scenes I was dreaming of consisted of me making a mad dash across a Blackjack table and grabbing a hand full of chips before running out the nearest exit or hoping for some panicked state of affairs that would lead to chips sprawled out all over the place giving me the opportunity to scoop some up on my way out the door. This would become my every Sunday routine.

When classes started the next day, I could not wait. It was the first day of graduate school, and I had waited a long time to get back in the classroom, although I could not imagine for the life of me that it would be under these circumstances. Nevertheless, this is what I had signed up for and wandered around hopelessly in the Nevada desert for, and it was finally my time. My plan was to specialize in political theory with a second specialty in American government. With my background in African American studies, I knew I was going to conduct research and write my thesis around the concept of racial politics, although there was no one in the department who specialized in that area or taught any classes in that field. No other student was doing research in this area at the time, which I had put in my application regarding my interests and plans when studying there. This helped to distinguish me and my research from that of the other students. Similar to my experience at Puget Sound, I immediately sought out a professor specializing in political theory; again, I was going to need a mentor. Sure, I had my own philosophy and way of doing things, but there was still a lot to learn about academia, and I was not going to make the same mistake I had made as an undergraduate regarding the process of graduate school and getting a PhD.

Dr Ring was the resident specialist in political theory, and I had signed up for all her classes that first semester. She was an older Jewish lady from the University of California-Berkeley, which had a reputation for social and student activism back in the 1960s as part of the Free Speech Movement. Although I was unfamiliar with the history of Berkeley at the time, it was not long before I was exposed to the ultra-liberal progressivism that the campus was known for. If anyone was going to be able to stomach a pro-Black social, cultural, and political stance from one of the graduate students, she was likely going to be the best candidate in the department. During our first meeting, I told her that I wanted to get my PhD in political science and teach about the Black political experience. She expressed the stereotypical liberal enthusiasm regarding anything that was "diverse" or nontraditional in political scope and showed me a couple of books from her shelf that she recommended that I read. For that whole first semester, I was at her side, attending every class and hanging out in her office during office hours. I had learned from all of the lessons from my undergraduate days and was now ready to unload at this new institution. I was more than confident in my intellectual abilities and had fine-tuned my ability to interact socially; I no longer had any doubts or fear of speaking in class and was more than prepared to reinvent myself. I was going to be a brilliant pain in the ass!

The conditions and atmosphere surrounding the department of political science certainly lent themselves to my plan to be an invaluable problem. There was only one other Black graduate student in the department who was from Belize and who had been there a year working as a graduate assistant. It did not take long to realize that to survive, blend in, and make friends with the other graduate students she had resigned herself to not expressing any particular pro-Black views or not identifying herself explicitly as a Black person. There were no Black professors in the department, and I don't recall having one Black professor during the entire two years I spent at the university. And no Black student entered the department before I left.

The whole time I never let on to anybody that I was homeless. Whenever people asked where I lived, I just said, "across town, but not too far." I ingratiated myself with the staff and faculty in the department by attending every orientation, welcome event, and lunch lecture that was offered. Whether I was interested in the people or the topic or not, I took advantage of the opportunity to get a free meal and would occasionally circle back after the event had ended and scoop up whatever leftovers remained into my backpack to eat later in my van or the next day. The cost of tuition included access to the student recreation center, which consisted of a gym with a locker room and showers. So every day before classes would start, I would shower and get dressed alongside the other students in the rec center, but I had no access to laundry or anything; thus, you can imagine returning back to the van daily to a duffle bag full of dirty clothes.

Every day I had the same routine: get up and go to the gym and shower, followed by attending whatever classes I had that day, concluding with hanging around the department of political science looking for any possible food or anyone going to get food that I might be able to get in on. When that failed, rather than hang out in my van, I would stay in the library every night until it closed to do homework and stream whatever TV that was available at the time. When the library closed, I drove my van back to the parking spot a few miles away to sleep. In the mornings before class, I would drive over to a casino that I had previously cased for free donuts from their poker room or on the floor for gambling patrons. Having no money, I would strategically sit down at a slot machine where a waitress was circling and act like I was playing; just randomly hitting the bet button or acting like I was changing the setting on the machine. When there was no time for that, I would walk into the poker room and sign up for the morning tournament, grab a donut, and pretend like I was walking around waiting for the tournament to start.

This routine was sustainable until one evening I decided to drive to a casino to watch Monday Night Football. On my way back to my parking spot at the truck stop, I got pulled over by the police on Highway 395. The van had a busted taillight, and I had taped on a red dishrag as its replacement. As per the standard, I gave the officer my license and registration. For some reason, I assumed that he was just checking my information, although as I was watching the other cars on the highway speed by, I realized that it was starting to take an unusually long time. When he finally came back, he said that the vehicle identification number on the registration did not match the number on the vehicle. As he was approaching my window with his flashlight, he could not help but notice that the back of the van was clearly my residence, with all the clothes, pillows, sleeping bag, and all. The officer said he could not legally let me drive the van with those license plates on the vehicle, but he would do me a favor and not tow the van. While being appreciative that all my possessions were going to be OK for the time being, I could not help but wonder what the purpose of taking the license plates was. The officer asked if I had a screwdriver. When I told him no, he walked back to his car, coming back with a flathead screwdriver in his hand. He really expected me to take these license plates off, which I rightfully possessed, right there on the side of the highway with cars passing by. All I could do while kneeling down to remove the license plates was to be thankful that the cop had stayed to take them in his possession because I was holding my breath the entire time. I had heard horror stories.

After I had removed the license plates and given them to the officer, I sat in the car for a moment to see if he was going to pull onto the highway ahead of me but after a while, noticing that he was still behind me, I figured it was best to just get off the freeway. But where was I going to go now? The truck stop was a few miles from campus, but that was going to be impossible to do every morning and night without license plates. This development only left me with one safe option to get to class each day without the risk of being pulled over to and from the university: parking near campus. The university was surrounded by student housing, hotels, and Greek row housing. There was no way I was going to risk parking in a casino parking lot every night. Instead, I decided to park just one street over from campus outside a student housing apartment complex. My rationale was that students probably had friends over that stayed the night and would park on the street there, so being ticketed or towed was of low probability, despite the fact that the car had no license plates. As I was driving, I could not help but think, first, that I was being set up and that this cop or one of his colleagues was going to stop me down the road a little way for not having a license plate. Or second, that the cop who pulled me over, knowing that I was not going to be able to make it very long with no license plates, was just doing me a short-term favor and was going to let some other cops be the real villain by towing away my residence with all my possessions.

That first night I could not sleep one bit. I had made a terrible miscalculation regarding my ability to sleep this close to campus and to where the students would routinely pass by at all hours of the night, returning home from a night out. The weekends were obviously the worst, but on weekdays there was barely any relief from the fear of someone walking up on me while I was trying to sleep. Since I could no longer depend on the free casino donuts, campus events and department lectures became even more vital. I attended every one. What I lacked in food, money, and resources I made up for in work ethic. I had nothing left to do but attend every class, read every book, and take notes upon notes. When I wasn't in class or sleeping in my van, I was in the library. This undoubtedly made me a very successful student and one that could be counted on to have any assignments thoroughly complete and available for the other students to ask questions. Not only was I excelling, but I was making myself useful. I was outspoken, challenging professors and other classmates, but never to the point of alienation.

There were two important lessons that I carried over from my undergraduate studies: first, never take a class that you don't need or aren't interested in, and second, never write a paper you can't use. One of the first things I did before even attending the university was to go through the course offerings and class catalog to see exactly what classes were required and when they were offered. I looked hard at the overview of the program to have an idea of the timing and where I needed to be at the end of each semester. Since I had planned on going forward to complete the PhD, I knew that by the second semester I would need to have more on my academic and research resume than I currently had. Looking ahead to PhD programs meant I had exactly two years, and I was not going to waste any time. Knowing what I wanted to write my master's thesis about was a big help. Since I had a general idea that I was going to investigate race and politics, in addition to the required courses, I took more philosophy courses as electives in order to further improve my ability to reason and develop my own arguments. In every paper I wrote in every class, I made sure that it related in some way to the issues of race and politics. This would be helpful in developing my thesis and, ultimately, I was able to incorporate into it whole pages from various papers written throughout the two years.

# My breaking point

Although I knew I was going to eventually write a thesis relating to the concepts of race and politics in America, I had nothing specific in mind or a strong political position to argue, certainly nothing that was on the academic radar. The only thing I knew for sure was that I planned on centering the conversation around the Black American experience in American politics. It was broad and it was vague, but I knew I had time to figure it out as I gathered material based on course reading and from the discussions and arguments that were taking place in class. As the only Black person in many of these classes, I made it a point to inquire how the issue being discussed pertained to or affected Black people, many times to the chagrin of my classmates. But unlike my undergraduate days, where I was most likely to keep these positions to myself, I was now extremely confident and well-read enough to tear into the other students.

The breaking point came in one of the many arguments between me and my adviser during one of our many back and forths during her office hours. I was taking my typical pro-Black stance in the spirit of Malcolm X and Huey Newton; she was taking her typical Berkeley progressive multicultural/diversity stance. I kept telling her, "multiculturalism screws Black people!" She then uttered a word that would come to haunt me for the rest of my academic career: "race is just a social construct." "What are you talking about!?" I responded back critically, "that's insane." Little did I know that she was about to give me a lesson in critical race theory, in that race as a social construct was their biggest sticking point. I had to know more about where this gross declaration had come from, so she gave me a list of books by Derrick Bell, Kimberlé Crenshaw, and Richard Delgado. Bell's *And We Are Not*

*Saved* and *Faces at the Bottom of the Well* are amazing works and became foundational in how I looked at institutional racism and also spurred my interest in psychoanalysis. The primary assumption of psychoanalysis is the belief that all people possess unconscious thoughts, feelings, desires, and memories (Shapiro, & Emde, 1991).

Thus it became important to me to know not only what decisions were made but why the people in power made the decisions that they did. I started reading biographies and watching documentaries on historical figures throughout history, paying extra attention to their family dynamics and the major events in their youth. Additionally, I started paying closer attention to my own mental state and growing psychosis as I maneuvered in what can only be described as a tormented mental state. I was poor and homeless in an area where people literally traveled from all over the world to spend and waste money. On a daily basis, I literally watched people throw money away and eat some of the finest cuisines while I survived on leftovers. I couldn't help but take note of what the conditions of homelessness and poverty while going to graduate school was doing to my own desires and growth and began to take the necessary steps to correct them.

As a person who relied heavily on, both personally and academically, nothing but sheer will, if nothing else, this method of investigating people's actions and political behavior became foundational to my approach. At the root of what would become my first philosophical inquiry would be society's overreliance on emotionalism over intellectualism and reasonable decision-making. As I fretted over this idea at night in my van when I couldn't sleep, I kept running into a wall in regard to why most people would continually practice habits that completely contradict what they claim are their social and political desires or aspirations. Thinking back to the liberal, progressive movement in Portland and all my white liberal friends in college, I wondered where the heart of their contradictions laid? It was in their unconscious thoughts and, most certainly, in their unspoken feelings, desires, and memories. The histories of their upbringings, how they were raised, and their socialization processes growing up played a major factor in American politics. It was not as easy as going into some voting booth and pulling the lever and, more increasingly, this is what political science had come to: an overemphasis on statistics and numbers and reading exit polls to make grand conclusions about the American state of political affairs and the human condition. It was as if political scientists were living in the 1800s and were expecting the American public to openly provide their deep-rooted racism and hatred for Black people in exit polls. This also drew me to the conclusion that politics in particular, as it concerned race and the historical experiences of Black people, meant that it was important to support not only people who looked like me but who also grew up similarly to how I did. I did not want to get into a race versus class debate because I was certainly going to champion the side of race every time, but look at the living conditions of poor whites, for example. However, there was also a certain level of oppression experienced by being poor and Black. Then add being poor and Black in predominately white places and spaces where the white liberal is always claiming to be your ally but is absent when needed the most. I believed that this was particularly psychologically damaging to African Americans. This phenomenon was to be described as "the racist you know versus the racist you don't know."

Nothing frustrated me more as a discipline outside of the deep-rooted racism within political science than the behavioral revolution. The behavioral revolution of the 1950s and early 1960s is a foundational moment in the history of political science and is widely considered to be a time when the discipline shed its traditional roots and embraced its identity as a modern social science. Many of the objects of study have not changed much since the 1930s, as political scientists have long studied power, the Presidency, Congress, the Supreme Court, voting behavior, public opinion, international relations, and comparative government (Adcock & Bevir, 2005). But in *The Political System: An Enquiry into the State of Political Science*, David Easton lectured his contemporaries about the failures of traditional political theory and the need for the development of general theory, such as the type of systems theory he developed to explain the workings of the US political system (Easton, 1951: 51). In *The Political System*, Easton expresses this desire to create a general theory of politics that is expressed in the language of adopting the scientific method and "a scientific approach to social knowledge." A decade later, Robert Dahl in his classic 1961 APSR article, "The Behavioral Approach in Political Science: Epitaph for a Monument to a Successful Protest," declared the ultimate victory of behavioralism over the subjective identities and practices of political science (Dahl, 1961).

Similarly, Schaar and Wolin open their critique by saying that "the study of politics has become increasingly scientific: that is, behavioral, quantitative, empirically oriented, experimental where possible, rigorous, and precise." In his article, "Political Theory: Evolution of a Sub-Field," Gunnell makes the relationship between the subfield of political theory and behavioralism clear and, again in his 1993 book, *The Descent of Political Theory: The Genealogy of an American Vocation*. Gunnell shows that the subfield of political theory has embraced an identity based on what are, in his view, two incompatible goals: the theory of politics and its practice. Here, in Gunnell's view, the subfield has been alienated from the discipline, the public, and itself. Gunnell recounts how the behavioral movement led to the marginalization of the subfield of political theory, which increasingly became isolated from the mainstream of the discipline. In "Political Science," Robert Adcock and Mark Bevir note how "the curtains were rising on what has come to be known as the 'behavioral revolution,' in which a movement of scholars set out to make political science more 'systematic' by transforming both its methods and theories" (Adcock & Bevir, 2005: 74).

This movement toward numbers and statistics and away from taking normative stances on political issues moved me closer and closer to political theory and further away from traditional political science. As a Black person, I kept thinking that this shift toward numbers and statistics in politics would further disenfranchise and alienate Black people. As long as people believed in the notion of American democracy, Black Americans would always be the victim of a numerical disadvantage, thus allowing whites to cover their racism with "that's just how the system of American democracy works." How could Blacks expect to get anything as a numerical minority when all people cared about essentially was maintaining the integrity of the US political system? Democracy was not going to help Black people, and now it had found a co-conspirator within the discipline of political science, which was now going to use statistics and numbers to justify the mistreatment and further oppression of Black people. I always hated the saying, "you can make numbers say anything," but now it had become abundantly clear that I had gotten involved with a discipline that was taking full advantage of it at the expense of people that not only looked like me but also who grew up like me.

And this is, again, where the core concepts of critical race theory (CRT) and the readings by Bell and Crenshaw were vital: America's institutions, both economic and political, were inherently racist, and racism played a significant role in the behavior of whites and how they saw African Americans' participation in American government. Overall, I agreed with many of CRT's points, except for the idea of race as a social construct. It was a dangerous concept that gave too much power and influence on humans who have demonstrated too many times our inability to handle such complicated issues. It argues that the Black "race" was constructed by society. Which begs the question, what society is responsible for constructing Black people as we know them? In American society, this would undoubtedly be the white dominant majority who has ruled and governed the social, political, and economic institutions since the founding. I was unwilling to give white people that much credit. Additionally, "construct" implies the possibility of deconstruction. So how do we go about deconstructing Black people? And deconstruct race down to what? The literature and discussion surrounding critical race theory and its claim that race is a social construct sounded eerily familiar to the progressive, liberal rhetoric that I had experienced my entire life: rather than acknowledge the unique and distinct history, culture, and experience of Black Americans, rather than confront head-on the ignorance and delusion of racism and white superiority, the strategy moving forward was, "we're all one race: the human race." Rather than confront differences, the typical progressive liberal machine of universalism was once again trying to solve the nation's problems by making everyone the same. I've seen this strategy play out before with the abolitionist movement, then the labor movement, then the civil rights movement, and all of these movements of trying to unite Americans under the guise of "sameness" met the same fate: white people in America have no interest in being the "same" as anybody, especially Black Americans. Any notion or feeling of comradery was short-lived, and the "we're all one race, human race" discussion went nowhere when it came to addressing the past injustices suffered by Black people in America. What Black people needed was not more inclusion, integration, and feelings of "sameness." Instead, the more effective strategy was separate and distinct institutions for Black Americans. This would mean a certain level of reliance on the concept of race to separate our needs and aspirations from the rest of the country, which due to our unique history, culture, and experience, was more than valid. Pushing and slowly eliminating another group's identity and culture in order to fit into the white American dominant majority was no victory, and it pained me to see the discourse around race and Blackness going down this troubled path. Thus, my master's thesis was aimed directly at this issue.

One of the most important developments in writing my thesis and the best overall experiences during graduate school that really gave me better insight into the future of academic writing and research was attending academic conferences. In the Spring of 2008, with a thesis project in construction, I decided to utilize the funding programs that the university had in place for graduate students to attend conferences. This would usually include registration fees, the cost of travel, and the hotel. Feeling like I had run into the brick wall of racial thought at my own university, I decided to take my ideas on the road, thinking that I might receive a more open-minded and receptive reaction. By the end of 2008, I had attended the Midwest Political Science Association National Conference in Chicago and the Western and Northwestern Political Science Association Annual Conferences in Vancouver, BC, and Portland, Oregon. In all instances, I was the only person from the department that attended, and I took the same paper to each one, a draft of what would become my thesis. I traveled to each place alone and had no prep or advice from anyone on what to expect from such an experience. Not only was it my first time presenting my own research, but it was also my first time being in many of these cities. Originally, I thought that being accepted into one of these conference programs was a big deal until I was let in on the secret that pretty much every submission was granted a platform in one academic category or the other. But for a first-time graduate student who had no experience, it felt good to believe that I had somehow accomplished something by the opportunity.

My research had gotten accepted in two categories: political theory and the up-and-coming politics of race. Racial politics was a relatively new category that many of the political science associations, as well as departments across the country, had flatly ignored or previously felt was insignificant to the political discourse of the time. But by now, word had spread of an upcoming politician from Chicago named Barack Obama, who was a senator from Illinois, but was slowly becoming the favorite for the Democratic Party's nominee for US president. In what seemed like a blink of an eye, there was an outpouring of new research and political inquiry into what the potential of a Black president meant for traditional studies of American politics. Thus, my research seemed to be making its appearance for the first time during a very favorable moment in American political history. While everyone was rushing to point out how Obama had the potential to bring the nation together in healing around the issue of race, here I came, young and inexperienced, throwing heavy critiques at this emerging field of racial politics and its goal of inclusivity and political integration.

Looking back, I have no idea what gave me the impression that the goal of dismantling progressive racial politics was achievable at academic conferences. Nevertheless, I felt obligated to take my ideas and theories on the road and try them out outside of my immediate area. But I knew nothing of the conference experience. Since I didn't know anyone, after registration, I skipped out on any events or mixers that would require me to interact with other people. Instead, I took the conference programs, found myself trying to figure out when and where I would be presenting, and looked for any other interesting topics or papers I was interested in hearing about, of which there were very few. After that, I spent the majority of my time traveling and experiencing these cities for the first time and seeing the sites.

Although I was prepared to present my research, I was ill-prepared to present my research at these conferences. Yes, I was looking for some insight and help on issues that I may have missed or ways to make my paper better. What I got was being continually shredded apart by people in the audience who questioned my audacity to go against what was now considered to be objective truth around the issues of race: it was a social construct. Furthermore, they said that I was going down a dangerously racist road by implying anything natural or inherent when discussing race or Blackness. And yet, I was used to people disagreeing with me and standing on my own intellectual island, so the ferocity and intensity with which the shots from the audience kept coming did not deter my stance on the topic or change the direction of the paper whatsoever. There were a few occasions when a member of the audience would stick around after the presentations were over and attempt to engage in discussion with me about my topic. The white members couldn't care less about my critique of race as a social construct and were much more curious about what I was trying to prove with my conclusion that Black people needed their own social, political, and economic institutions. The few Black members of the audience would attempt to pull me to the side and advise me to tread lightly. They were amazed that I was not only in attendance at the conference by myself, but would ask me where my adviser or mentor was during this whole process. Why would they send me out there to present this type of research alone? Rather than feeling dejected, I took note of every critique and took them home to address every one of them in my paper. In the end, these conferences served as litmus tests for how I believed the rest of my scholarship would be received due to the fact that I planned to investigate what, I believed, would be much more difficult topics than this one. Attending academic conferences had served its purpose, and I was ready to go back to Nevada and finish what I had started.

By the time I returned for my final year of graduate school at Nevada, the frustration with my department and the reception that I was getting on campus had me ready to leave. Whereas I originally planned to stay and finish my PhD at Nevada, where I had started graduate work, by August of 2008 it was clear that I had overstayed my welcome, and there was no point in even applying to stay in the program. Political theory was continuing its decline in prominence, and the lack of intellectual rigor of the other students in the program left me dissatisfied. I began getting a reputation for walking out of classes in disgust and for continually getting into verbal sparring matches with other students in the program. It had gotten to the point where even my own adviser had asked me to stop coming to class. My presence, she said, was not conducive to the success of the other students in class, and she promised to give me a grade no lower than a B+ if I would stop coming to the graduate political theory section. A graduate seminar usually consists of five to ten students who meet once a week for three hours and is meant to be more in-depth and rigorous than a traditional undergraduate section. Additionally, most graduate students, by this point, should be somewhat familiar with the basic texts in political theory, allowing for much deeper analysis and critique. Instead, what I found was the class being taught to the lowest intellectual level, with little to no discussion and with time being used to walk through each text as if these were first-time readers. What I had hoped would finally be a grown-up discussion around the concepts of justice and virtue became an undergraduate course held later on in the day. That's it; that was the only distinction between this graduate seminar and an intro class full of freshmen. Once again, the intellectual bar was being lowered to the most menial minds and trains of thought. Students who had studied little and written even less were being heralded around the department as up-and-coming, while those who had been working and producing in the department without routinely brownnosing other faculty and staff were on the outside looking in. Once again, it was the concept of meritocracy and achievement on what you had accomplished instead of whom you knew and whether your ideas conformed with the mainstream ones. And now, with no adviser or mentor, my final days as a graduate student in Nevada were spent pleading with whatever faculty left in the department that I could find and who I had not offended in some way to sit on my master's committee. I had already been admitted to a PhD program with no congratulatory reaction of any kind, and I just needed to put together a committee to review my thesis. On my last day I left the department arguing with the chair on how it even came to that point in the first place. They continually backed and supported people who had little to no experience and had no rigorous research prospectus or innovative ideas. And these people were passed through the program with little obstruction, and many received their congratulatory flowers on the way out. I left the University of Nevada without ever going back to my office or attending graduation.

# Finish the job: Howard and the PhD

When it came time to finish my PhD, I could not wait to finally dive much deeper into my interests in racial politics, especially as it concerned the Black political experience. Originally, I had hoped to attend UCLA, where my then-adviser Dr Ring had recommended that I go to work alongside her adviser when she was a graduate student, and who had also done some research on racial politics and published works on Malcolm X. Still homeless, I had to ask my family for money so that I could drive all the way to UCLA from Reno just to meet Dr Wolfenstein. I had risked everything in the dead of winter just to sit on this man's couch for about an hour, just to turn around and drive back to Reno, starving and almost running out of gas in the process. But when it came time to apply, my fractured relationship with my own adviser, who had by now asked me to stop attending class, had assuredly become well-known, and what had once seemed a sure thing was now completely off the table. But unlike the first time applying to graduate school, I was well-prepared.

Once again, I knew exactly what my proposed area of study was going to be, and I even had a dissertation topic already worked out. I had learned my lesson from applying to the University of Nevada and checked every box, declaring that a fellowship that would assure my funding was a requirement of my acceptance. No more just looking to get in somewhere. This time I was looking to go somewhere I could thrive and unapologetically explore and unleash the full range of my intellectual abilities without having to limit or restrain myself. I also wanted to take advantage of my experience while in Nevada and try moving somewhere else that

I had never been in the hope of having one more opportunity to reinvent myself in a new place. But I had grown so frustrated with my experience in Nevada and the racial discourse taking place within national politics that I felt obligated to go outside the tradition and look for something else. Somewhere where I could completely explore and have discussions around the concept of race and Blackness without feeling like an outsider. Plus, I had had my fill of stereotypical traditional American government discourse and the same old arguments with white students about the founding fathers and how great America was. Predominantly white institutions had given me all that they could possibly afford me and nothing more, so I decided to attend Howard University in Washington, DC.

Howard University had the reputation of being the elite historically Black college and university. It had awarded doctorates to more Black people in America than any other university and was located in America's political capital. Perhaps, the greatest factor contributing to my affinity for Howard was not that it was over 90 percent Black, but that its political science department had a specialty in Black politics. There was no other institution in the country that I found which had a graduate specialty in Black politics, and that was all it took for me to go there. Howard also had a specialty in political theory, so I could not imagine a more perfect fit for my academic and intellectual pursuits than the political science department at Howard University.

At the same time, nothing expanded my intellectual reach and research concerns more than my time spent at Howard. For the first time, there was no mention of the American founding fathers or any white American political theorist outside of the undergraduate-level introduction to political theory class. There was no mention of any major significant white philosophers or political theorists either. To mention one would immediately give you the skeptical side eye around the intellectual students in the departments. If anything, the majority of conversations surrounding many of the theorists that I was raised and groomed on from an undergraduate student through my master's degree experience were aimed at denouncing their ideas and influence while noting a prominent Black intellectual who was much more influential. Every single class that I took for two years of coursework was all Afrocentric, centering the Black African experience first and foremost. It was completely different to my previous graduate and undergraduate experiences. Outside of the majority of faculty, students, and staff being Black, the surrounding culture of Washington, DC felt like an immersion in Black culture. Just walking off the metro to walk to campus, you could routinely hear the sound of native DC go-go music playing from a local barbershop. There was no campus community where I felt more at home than being around Howard University and living in northeast DC.

There is no doubt that I owe much of my current success in Black Studies to my days at Howard University. It was the first time that I had ever heard of or read of Black philosophers and political theorists. Specializing in Black Politics and Political theory introduced me to so many texts that are now part of my teaching regimen and philosophical catalog. I remember reading Cornel West and Tommie Shelby and thinking if only I had had these readings and concepts previously, it would have saved me a lot of frustration while equipping me with a healthy artillery against my white counterparts. The international relations course I took centered on the influences and conflict of colonialism in Africa while barely mentioning the social, economic, and political institutions and governments of other nations. Whereas colonialism had never come up in any of my previous coursework, I certainly had learned about the different types of democracies in European countries. The concept of white nationalism was introduced to me through the writing of Ronald Walters, and before he passed away, I even got the chance to meet him at a research panel held at the founder's library on Howard's campus. Partnered with the works of Charles Mills, in particular *The Racial Contract*, I was quickly learning more about institutional racism and the study of whiteness in all aspects of American government and global capitalism. Even my contentious relationship with faith was affected by my experience at Howard as I was introduced to the liberating theology of James Cone which, once again, changed how I looked at practicing what was left of my faith at the time.

Additionally, I was introduced to more Black African theorists and African historians that I would have never come across at any of my previous institutions and would have been ridiculed for even suggesting them. Before long, I had met and become good friends with a great group of colleagues who shared much of the same revolutionary spirit, deeply rooted in pro-Blackness and African history. Many of the books and theorists that I came to be introduced to came straight off the bookshelves of my closest friends. How I had even made it this far in academia and focusing on the Black experience without reading or understanding these texts was shocking to them, and I could not wait to catch up, and they were eager to help me catch up to speed as well. Ivan Van Sertima's *They Came Before Columbus*, Chancellor Williams's *Destruction of Black Civilization*, John G. Jackson's *Christianity Before Christ*, Yosef ben-Jochannan's *Black Man of the Nile* and *African Origins of the Major Western Religions*, and George G. M. James's *Stolen Legacy* completely blew my mind wide-open and made me completely question everything thought I knew about the world, religion, and history. All of a sudden, there was a new joy and pride I felt discovering all these new concepts and forgotten histories of Blackness. I felt that I had been lied to and misled by all my other institutions. How come nobody was teaching this stuff!? Part of me felt vindicated for so many arguments and areas of contention at my previous schools, while the other part of me felt like I had been done an extreme disservice but was about to spend the rest of my life making up for it. There was so much to learn that I had completely ignored while doing traditional American government and political science.

The majority of my time spent at Howard University consisted of reading. There were so many books and authors that I was exposed to on that campus and, once again, I found myself in a new city where I did not know many people. Additionally, with two specializations in which I would need to take and pass comprehensive exams in, Black Politics and Political Theory, there was plenty of reading to keep me busy on top of my coursework and dissertation research and preparation. A comprehensive exam is an evaluation that measures a student's competency and mastery of concepts in the field of an academic discipline. The purpose of the comprehensive exam is to ensure that the student is knowledgeable enough about his or her area of research to make an original contribution. My third specialty was American government, but I was not required to test in that, which was a huge benefit. Plus, I had essentially been studying American government my whole life and had already been teaching it; what was going to make me the academic and professor I wanted to be was in Black theory, which I had been doing since my first days as an undergraduate student. But now that I had been introduced to and fully immersed in Black political thought, I believed that this combination of specialties would be best to set me apart and give me the best opportunity to get a job in political science when I was done.

## Conclusion

By the end of my first year, I had lost my adviser, this time to another job in the area at American University. She was the only white woman in the department, and it certainly did not do her or me any favors to be working together while in that department. She was the main political theorist in the department, so it only made sense that we worked together. I was extremely hard-working, and she did her best to advise me to keep my head down, complete my coursework, and "get the hell out of here as soon as possible." Taking that advice only seemed to make matters worse. Similar to my experience at the University of Nevada, without an adviser or mentor, I was left on my own to fend for myself and navigate the entire dissertation process on my own, including finding a dissertation committee. As a result, with few courses left, I spent less and less time on campus and in the halls around the department. With all my time and energy focused on the process of completing my PhD and the fact that I was already teaching at a nearby community college, my character began to take a hit which only made me heed the words of my adviser to "get the hell out" of there as soon as possible. By the end of my time at Howard, I had completed my dissertation and received my degree in the mail, just like at the University of Nevada. I had officially finished my student experience upon the completion of my PhD, and at each institution, I had left with a bad taste in my mouth, very little to no recognition, no faculty support or advice, and no need to return after it was all over.

# 3

# Beef with America's founding fathers

Perhaps the biggest recollection that framed my political thought and understanding of the ills of American government came directly from the mouth of the founding fathers themselves. As a student of political science in the US, there is no escaping the reach and bounds to which white Americans will go to defend and praise them. Therefore, there has been no bigger villain or aim of my academic and intellectual frustration than with the founding fathers and America's hypocritical and delusional relationship with them. The relationship white America has with the founding fathers has been an immovable force throughout political discourse in the US, and as a student, and professor, there has been no greater opponent. To be clear, I have no doubts about the accomplishment of the American Revolution, and no doubts that many of the founding fathers were very intelligent men and leaders in their particular fields or industries. I have no beef with the quest for freedom and fleeing from religious persecution, although religious persecution is highly overstated and mostly an inaccurate argument concerning the founding of America. But let's be clear, the founding fathers ushered in one of the worst political disasters in human history.

Slaves and slavery are mentioned only indirectly in the 1787 Constitution. For example, Article 1, Section 2, Clause 3 prescribes that "three-fifths of all other Persons" are to be counted for the apportionment of seats in the House of Representatives and direct taxes. Additionally, in Article 4, Section 2, Clause 3, slaves are referred to as "persons held in service or labor." The founding fathers, however, did make important efforts to contain slavery. Many northern states had adopted legislation to end or significantly reduce slavery during and after the American Revolution. In 1782 Virginia passed a manumission law that allowed slave owners to free their slaves by will or deed. As a result, thousands of slaves were manumitted in Virginia. Thomas Jefferson, in 1784, proposed to ban slavery in all the Western Territories, which failed to pass Congress by one vote. Partially following Jefferson's plan, Congress did ban slavery in the Northwest Ordinance of 1787 for lands north of the Ohio River. The international slave trade was banned in all states except South Carolina by 1800. Finally, in 1807, President Jefferson called for and signed into law a federally enforced ban on the international slave trade throughout the US and its territories. It became a federal crime to import or export a slave. However, the domestic slave trade allowed for the expansion and the diffusion of slavery into the Louisiana Territory. Slavery would not eventually end until Congress passed the 13th Amendment in 1865.

The founding fathers were either racists, white supremacists, or both, who have said some of the most harmful and degrading things about Black people in this country. Thomas Jefferson is the quintessential figure in authoring America's declaration to the world and also its racial contract. The author of the Declaration of Independence, a preeminent intellectual and acquaintance through correspondence of the African American intellectual Benjamin Banneker, Jefferson was a racist white supremacist (Walton, Smith, & Wallace, 2017: 8). Merrill Peterson, a biographer of Thomas Jefferson, wrote that his remarks were "thinly disguised folk beliefs about Negroes" (Peterson, 1970: 262). In his "Notes on the State of Virginia," he summarily dismissed the accomplishments of two contemporary Black writers, Phyllis Wheatley and Ignatius Sancho. He added that to justify his general conclusions on Blacks requires many observations of a scientific nature that had not been undertaken in his study. He also confessed that "to our reproach, it must be said that though for a century and a half, we have had under our eyes the races of black and red men, they have never been viewed by us as subjects of natural history" (Jefferson, 1998: 143). Having made no observations of a scientific nature, you would think Mr Jefferson would refrain from making sweeping generalizations about Africans that would impact the course of history and the foundation of the democratic experiment taking shape in the newly formed US. Yet, in his Notes, Jefferson declares:

> Comparing them by their faculties of memory, reason, and imagination, it appears to me that in memory, they are equal to the whites; in reason, much inferior, as I think one could scarcely be found capable of tracing and comprehending the investigations of Euclid; and that in imagination they are dull, tasteless, and anomalous. It would be unfair to follow them to Africa

for this investigation. We will consider them here, on
the same stage as the whites and where the facts are
not apocryphal on which a judgment is to be formed.

(Ibid. 155)

Having no observations of a scientific nature to rely on, Jefferson's words echo throughout our current political climate. Declaring Blacks inferior in reason and, therefore, inferior to whites is one of the most impactful statements in world history and has had the biggest, most negative impact on the history of Africans in America. Remember, their American experiment was supposed to be founded in liberal ideology and democratic theory that emphasizes that we humans are naturally in a perfect state of freedom to order our actions as we see fit. Through our ability to reason, democracy becomes a desirable form of government. Due to our ability to reason, we can decide for ourselves whom to grant political authority over the state in a limited form. Jefferson seems to ignore the basic premise of his own beliefs by declaring Blacks inherently inferior, but by tracing their inferiority to a lack of reason, he justified their inability to be equal participants in the newly formed republic. His use of reason to assist in the claim of Black inferiority is integral to the failed experiment of the American republic.

Jefferson's corruption of freedom and justice did not end there. Making Blacks inferior in reason and therefore unable to be equal participants in the republic was only the beginning. To truly set up a white supremacist society with institutional racism embedded within it, you need more than just the inferiority of reason to truly make it stick. There were arguably plenty of whites in the South that could certainly be less qualified in reason than many of the

Blacks Jefferson personally knew who were enslaved. Culturally, there needed to be an additional distinction between whites and Blacks, and Jefferson knew exactly what would help. About the condition of the Negro, he would add:

> The Negro, as already observed, exhibits the natural man in his completely wild and untamed state. We must lay aside all thought of reverence and morality—all that we call feeling—if we would rightly comprehend him; there is nothing harmonious with humanity to be found in this type of character… I advance it therefore as a suspicion only, that the blacks, whether originally a distinct race, or made distinct by time and circumstances, are inferior to the whites in the endowments both of body and mind.
>
> (Jefferson, 1998: 155)

One of the many claims that whites have used against Blacks in America is the belief that Blacks are naturally uncivilized and barbaric, coming from a dark continent with very little to contribute to the advancing society.

By declaring the wild and untamed state of the Negro and pleading with us to ignore the standards of morality, Jefferson was enabling those in the colonies, who were religious or people of strong faith, to be comfortable with the oppression and violent abuse aimed at the slaves. This use of religion, in particular, the white, Eurocentric version of Christianity, was vital to the perpetuation and sustenance of the violent abuse that Black people experienced during slavery. Scripture about the slaves being good to their masters and treating them with the same reverence as we would treat Christ and God himself! Could there be anything more damaging to the spirit and minds of Black people than to believe that they were worthy of the violent mistreatment that they were experiencing and that even the thought of revolting against their masters was a sin against God?

In 1790, during the debate over the slave trade, William Loughton Smith of South Carolina maintained that if slavery was a "moral evil," then it was "like many others which exist in all civilized countries, and which the world quietly submits to" (Annals of Congress, 1790: 1560). One Georgian Lutheran minister admitted that slavery was wrong "in the abstract," but then went on to justify it because it removed "the African from the heathenism of his native land to a country where his mind would be enlightened by the gospel, and provision made for the salvation of his soul..." (Weil, 2019). In other words, "the evils of slavery might be endured in the consideration of the moral and spiritual advantages which it bestows upon its unfortunate victims" (Bellot, 1971: 37). One Southerner claimed, for example, that God had permitted some of the Africans to be "dragged into bondage" so that they might learn from the experience and then return to Africa, taking with them "the light of civilization, and the blessings of Christianity, to their benighted and unhappy countrymen." Thus from this "apparent evil," God could bring about "the utmost possible good" (Staudenraus, 1961). Some preachers encouraged slave owners to allow their slaves to attend worship services—though only in separate gatherings led by white proslavery preachers. They had to be seated in the back or the balcony of segregated churches. Those men of God argued in their sermons on the injunction in Ephesians and Colossians that "slaves, obey your earthly master" would promote docility among enslaved workers. Some theologians said it was providence that had brought Africans to America as slaves since their enslavement would allow them to encounter the Christian message, and thus their eternal souls would be saved. Frederick Dalcho carried this argument one step further. He claimed that the New Testament required of servants "obedience, submission, [and] subjection, to a bad, as well as to a good master." Moreover, he insisted that there was "nothing in the law of God which can, in the slightest manner, justify the disobedience and revolt of slaves" (Rogers, 1985: 25). The South Carolina minister, Richard Furman, could insist that the "Christian Golden Rule: did not apply to slavery." "Surely this rule," he wrote, was "never to be urged against the order of things, which the Divine government has established" (Rogers, 1985: 8). Applied to slavery, the golden rule merely meant that the master should treat his slave as he would like to be treated if he were a slave. This same sentiment was echoed by Congressman Weems in January 1829.

To make certain no one missed the point, one pamphleteer explicitly linked the Mosaic law to the Africans. He contended that it was "highly probable that the Africans we enslave are descendants of the very same Heathen that were round about the Israelites." Since these Africans still remained unconverted and since the whites were "at least descended" from the Israelites, then the latter could enslave the former. "Will it be denied," he argued, "that we are entitled to the liberty of enslaving the Africans and the Heathen round about us also?" (Morrison, 1980: 20). One South Carolinian, writing in 1823, maintained that all the sophistry in the world cannot get rid of this decisive example.

Christianity robs no man of his rights, he argued. He went so far as to claim that this Epistle really sanctioned the fugitive slave law because "slaves should not be taken or detained from their master, without their master's consent" (ibid.: 22). They also maintained that slaveholding also received "negative sanction" in the Old Testament in that no place was there a passage of scripture that condemned or opposed slavery. God had spoken through his prophets for over two thousand years, and none of them had condemned or opposed the practice of holding slaves; slavery, therefore, had to be acceptable to God.

Ironically, at the same time, many whites were forbidding their slaves from learning how to read, from the contradictory belief that learning about the message and meaning behind many of the scriptures would lead the enslaved Blacks into rebellion. The Alabama Slave Code of 1833 included the following law: "Any person who shall attempt to teach any free person of color, or slave, to spell, read or write, shall upon conviction thereof by indictment, be fined in a sum of not less than two hundred fifty dollars, nor more than five hundred dollars." Slave narratives from many sources tell us how many enslaved people became educated. Some learned to read from other literate slaves, while at other times, a master or mistress was willing to teach a slave in defiance of the laws. Former slave and abolitionist leader Frederick Douglass was taught the alphabet in secret at age twelve by his master's wife, Sophia Auld. For those slaves who were able to read and given the Bible as their primary source, they were given a separate "Slave Bible" that omitted much of the New Testament.

# Racism in political science

The racist and white supremacist rhetoric throughout my studies of political science concerning the founding fathers and the foundation of the American experiment was not exclusive to political science alone. There were also remnants within my studies in philosophy, including G. W. F. Hegel who was the mentor to one of my personal favorites, Friedrich Nietzsche. Hegel would use similar rhetoric, perhaps borrowed from Jefferson himself, when Hegel discusses the wild and untamed state of the African. Hegel declares:

> In Negro life the characteristic point is that consciousness has not yet attained the realization of any substantial objective existence—as for example, God, or Law—in which the interest of man's volition is involved and in which he realizes his own being. This distinction between himself as an individual and the universality of his essential being, the African in the uniform, undeveloped oneness of his existence has not yet attained; so that the knowledge of an absolute Being, an Other and a Higher than his individual self, is entirely wanting. The Negro, as already observed, exhibits the natural man in his completely wild and untamed state.
>
> (Hegel, 1967: 93)

All fields of study within traditional American education have their moments of racism, and yet it never stopped me from continuing to pursue my studies and dive deeper into the readings and theories of the authors. It was not just in political science and my confrontation with the founding fathers that I encountered racist ideas and language from the theorists that I was learning from.

As an undergraduate and graduate student, I took a class on Marxism. In both instances, the entire 16 weeks were spent diving into the texts and theories of Marx and Engels. As a student, I was fascinated by a theoretical and practical alternative to capitalism which, from where I was standing, did not and could not work. Economic inequality was rampant. The rich were getting richer, and the poor were getting poorer. There was no meritocracy. I witnessed my mother work two or three jobs at a time to earn a living for three sons just to barely have enough, while people who did not work even half as hard as she did had more than enough. If working hard and pulling yourself up by your own bootstraps was the strategy, we should have been millionaires! No one outworked my mother. When I went to college and throughout my career, I tried to mirror her work ethic, only to find myself poor and living paycheck to paycheck as well. Being rich and having money by default opened the door to an alternative universe full of opportunities and experiences that poor people could only hope to achieve. Early on in my studies, we learned about economic inequality in America and the role of economic mobility. Economic mobility is the ability of an individual, family, or some other group to improve (or lower) their economic status—usually measured in income. Economic mobility is often measured by movement between income quintiles. Economic mobility may be considered a type of social mobility, which is often measured by change in income (Fields, 1996). Studies have shown that the majority of Americans live and die in the economic class that they were born into.

Meaning, if you were born poor, you are more likely to die poor, and vice versa. Well, this undoubtedly put the majority of Black people in America at an inherent disadvantage while giving whites an unearned disadvantage. And yet, we were expected to pull ourselves up by our own bootstraps when seemingly no one in America was capable of doing so and, certainly, the odds of doing so dramatically decreased while simultaneously confronting domestic terrorism at the hands of whites, coupled with institutional racism in all aspects of American life.

At no point before I got to college was I ever introduced to an alternative to capitalism and, yet, as a young Black male from a single-parent home, I was living all of the ills of a capitalist economic system and nearly none of the benefits. I was eager and hungry for an alternative theory that more closely explained the material conditions that I was experiencing and living through while analyzing the tools and institutional structures that reinforced Black oppression. I was certainly experiencing capitalism; rampant, unfettered materialism and individualism, the profit motive to get cash by any and all means necessary, commodity fetishism, and the constant need for new, brighter, fancier things to compare and fit in with friends and the rest of mainstream society. I absolutely begged and pleaded for my mother to buy me the material things that we surely could not afford, but that everyone at school was wearing and were, "oh, so trendy." It wasn't until I got to college that I realized that the constant need to impress others through the acquisition of material goods and money was part of the problem and not the solution to not only bettering my own existence, but also the material and political development of Black people in America.

By the time I got to college and was introduced to Marx, I was a poor college student doing everything in my power to live above my means and fit in at a private liberal arts university with students who were considerably wealthier than me. And yet, I was forced to prove my belonging through sheer work ethic and will without any material benefits to show for it. The discrepancies between wealth and the privilege that it provided were even more glaring in college than in high school, where at least some of the material conditions and displays of wealth by the students could be easily associated with their parents. But in college, we were on our own without parents; thus, the outward displays of wealth were much more closely associated with the individual student. It was not solely that their parents were buying them things, but that they simply had more money than me! And even while I was identifying with Marx's theories of alienation and the failures of capitalism, I couldn't help but be confronted with the racism throughout the economic system and Black people's ability to prosper economically. Marx commented with approval on the contention that Negroes had degenerated from a higher race (Paul, 1981). Both Marx and Engels sometimes used the English term "nigger" to refer to Blacks and to others for whom they had contempt. Ultimately, Marx's and Engels's public writings on the American Civil War are certainly sympathetic to the cause of "Negroes" (Padover, 1972: 39). The fact that Marx ultimately treated race and the experiences of Blacks so flippantly was troubling but did not take away from the ultimate message that I received from his theories. If anything, it reinforced my Black identity through the readings by locating the experience and oppression faced by African Americans at the root of Marxist theories. We were the real proletariat.

Marx was not the only theorist that I had to confront on my way to the founding fathers and on my way to discovering my own political identity. Nietzsche was another one and he used the term race for two different meanings: one for ethnic groups and one for social classes. He believed that race and class are identical in the sense that nations are composed of different races and that the upper classes are usually of a superior nature to the lower classes. One of the themes that Nietzsche often used to explain social phenomena was the mixing of races. He believed that mixed-race persons were usually inferior because of the conflicting, incompatible instincts that existed in them, and on these grounds he advocated for racial purification (Nietzsche, 1998 a and b). He blamed the mixing of the races on the decay of European society and culture. He also used the term "race" to mean ethnic group and, in this sense, he supported the idea of mixing specific races he considered to be of high quality. Despite Nietzsche's treatment of race, I treated his theories no differently than any other that I was reading at the time. If I was going to be primarily reading "old white males," then racist and ill-informed ideas and treatment of Black people was just something that I was going to have to get used to.

My treatment of the founding fathers was altogether different. They had reinforced their racist, white supremacist views with institutions. They had created an entire government based on the premise of their racist, white supremacist views. This was something much different from a general theory of economics and class that treated the Negro as insignificant at best. The founding fathers had literally gone out of their way to declare the Negro inferior and create an unfair system based on white supremacy. They then reinforced and codified their racism and feelings of white superiority through the constitution and the emphasis on the rule of law. Plus, many mainstream whites are not having intense debates about the failures of capitalism and the significance of individual will within the general discussions about the health and well-being of the American republic. Even today, contemporary discussions about Democrats being socialist and how important capitalism is to the success and future of America have nothing to do with race and Marx's views on Black people. In most instances, discussions around Marx and socialism are used to reinforce the institutional racism within capitalist America. The notion of redistributing wealth or of the federal government providing more economic opportunities to poor people and racial minorities is troubling and drives many whites deeper into their racist feelings of the inferiority of Blacks and the superiority of whites. They typically ask, "why does the federal government need to do more for them? Why can't they just pull themselves up by their own bootstraps like I did, and my grandfather did?" These are the debates and issues that Black people experience; not whether Marx and Nietzsche were racist. But with the founding fathers, there is no doubt. They were racist, white supremacists, and they built a nation based on those principles.

The racist, white supremacist thinking of the founding fathers lived well beyond their years and expanded into more realms than just the foundation and structure of the American republic. The treatment of Blacks in America is not confined to just the words of the founding fathers about slavery, or to how they treated slavery in the constitution, or to their private words expressed to friends and colleagues through their letters. The racist, white supremacist thinking of the founding fathers permeates through post-slavery America as it concerns what to do with Blacks once slavery inevitably ended. Post-slavery America and the rhetoric that surrounded the treatment and what to do with the newly freed Blacks is just as impactful and continues to resonate through contemporary America as much as the absence of freedom written in the constitution. Beginning in "Laws," Jefferson wrote:

> It will probably be asked, Why not retain and incorporate the blacks into the state, and thus save the expense of supplying, by importation of white settlers, the vacancies they will leave? Deep rooted prejudices entertained by the whites; ten thousand recollections, by the blacks, of the injuries they have sustained; new provocations; the real distinctions which nature has made; and many other circumstances, will divide us into parties, and produce convulsions which will probably never end but in the extermination of the one or the other race.

Here Jefferson has literally laid the groundwork for the continued oppression and disenfranchisement of Blacks. He sees no way in which Black people and white people can live and govern peacefully in America. Are we not witnessing this right now? Jefferson wrote the document that helped shape and form this nation; if anyone could speak to its purpose and potential, it would be him. And even as the chief architect of this American experiment, he sees no way in which this experiment works with Blacks and whites as equals.

Jefferson's reasoning is just as, if not more, important in explaining the ills and failures of the American government. At this point, I believe we can, unfortunately, look past the fear of the "ten thousand recollections by the Blacks." If those recollections, in addition to the hundreds of years of explicit and institutional racism since slavery ended, have not moved the Black community in America to consider alternatives to the current movement of status quo politics and capitalism, then perhaps nothing will. But more important is his belief in the "deep rooted prejudices entertained by whites." This comment is the hidden gem within the failures of the American experiment. What Jefferson is declaring is that even if Blacks were to somehow ignore their history of mistreatment and forego any notion of violent rebellion against whites, white people in America would never be able to get over historical feelings toward the Negro. And this is where we find ourselves today. This is what the insurrection on the Capitol in Washington, DC, on January 6, 2021, was all about. White Americans can and will never forget the centuries of American history when Black people were property, had no rights or privileges that white people had to respect, knew their place as second-class citizens, and the fact that their basic cultural, political, and economic institutions throughout America were built with the exclusive purpose of protecting and improving the conditions of white people.

No matter how much racial "equality" is achieved, no matter how much integration and inclusion in which Black people in America find themselves in the multitude of professions and institutions, and no matter if a Black person gets elected to the higher offices in the country, there is still no forgetting by white Americans that

Black people used to be beneath them and that at no point did the founding fathers think that they would be equal to whites in any way. What "make America great again" is about, more than anything, is this feeling among white Americans that somehow the traditional root of America is slowly slipping away from them. This is not the America they were raised in, learned about, and believed in from the beginning. The founding fathers wouldn't even recognize America anymore! White America demands and clamors for the times before when America was thriving, Black people knew their place, and white America will never forget where that place used to be and where they believe Blacks were meant to remain. There is no amount of education and anti-racist training that can erase the memories of whites and their historical standing in America and their treatment of Black people. There is no level of integration and interaction that can be achieved between whites and Blacks in America that can overcome the memories of whites as the "superior" race that was meant to civilize minorities on their way to complete control and domination over the basic institutions that impact and control daily American life. If Jefferson saw no way in which Blacks and whites could live and govern peacefully together in America as equals, then what possible solution to the American experiment is there that does not include the ultimate subjugation and disenfranchisement of one group or the other? If Blacks were not meant to be, or were incapable of becoming, integrated into American society as free people after slavery was abolished, even if due to no fault of their own other than the fact that because whites will never forget how terribly they treated them for hundreds of years, then Jefferson was left with no choice but to provide white America with an alternative blueprint of what to do in order to maintain the health and success of the American republic: get rid of the Negroes.

In 1821, five years before his death, Jefferson wrote that "nothing is more certainly written in the book of fate that these people are to be free, nor is it less certain that the two races, equally free, cannot live in the same government" (Walton, Smith, & Wallace, 2017: 62). He goes on to say, "My doubts on the competency of Blacks were the result of personal observation on the limited sphere of my own state where the opportunities for the development of their genius were not favorable, and those exercising it less so" (Magnis, 1999: 504). He hoped slavery would be abolished someday, but "when freed, he [the Negro] is to be removed beyond the reach of mixture" (Walton, Smith, & Wallace, 2017: 5). Ultimately, Jefferson was so convinced of the inferiority of Blacks and the deep-rooted prejudice of whites that the only reasonable solution that he could come up with was to remove the Negro from "beyond reach of mixture." If Blacks could not be removed from beyond reach, they could still not achieve the level of standing as that of whites. The history of the franchise reflects a clear conception of the US as a nation ruled by and for whites. Every state that entered the Union between 1819 and the Civil War denied Blacks the vote. The federal government prohibited free Blacks from voting in the territories it controlled. Abraham Lincoln considered Blacks to be—in his words— "a troublesome presence" in the US (Walton, Smith, & Wallace, 2017: 34).

During the Lincoln–Douglas debates, Lincoln stated: "I am not nor ever have been in favor of making voters or jurors of negroes, nor of qualifying them to hold office, nor to intermarry with white people; and I will say in addition to this that there is a physical difference between the white and black races which I believe will forever forbid the two races living together on terms of social and political equality" (Walton, Smith, & Wallace, 2017: 35). His opponent Stephen Douglas was even more outspoken: "For one, I am opposed to negro citizenship in any form. [Cheers—*Times*] I believe that this government was made on the white basis. ['Good,'—*Times*] I believe it was made by white men for the benefit of white men and their posterity forever, and I am in favor of confining the citizenship to white men—men of European birth and European descent, instead of conferring it upon negroes and Indians, and other inferior races" (Walton, Smith, & Wallace, 2017: 42). Throughout his presidency, Lincoln took the conventional view that if slaves were freed, they should be expatriated. Even in the midst of the war, he was making plans for colonization and appointed Reverend James Mitchell to be Commissioner of Emigration, with instructions to find a place to which Blacks could be sent. On August 14, 1862, Lincoln invited a group of free Black leaders to the White House to tell them, "There is an unwillingness on the part of our people, harsh as it may be, for you free colored people to remain with us" (Walton, Smith, & Wallace, 2017: 43). He urged them to lead others of their race to a colonization site in Central America.

Lincoln was the first president to invite a delegation of Blacks to the White House—and he did so to ask them to leave the country. Later that year, in a message to Congress, he argued not just for voluntary colonization but for the forcible removal of free Blacks. Even the Great Emancipator, Abraham Lincoln himself, the man credited for ending slavery and freeing the slaves, even he saw no way in which whites and Blacks could live together and govern together peacefully in America. The words of the founding fathers resonated with even the Great Emancipator. Giving Lincoln credit for the abolition of slavery and treating him as some great moral figure worthy of our admiration for racial justice and equality is even more troubling given the fact that emancipation was not his goal, but rather saving the Union and keeping the Confederacy from being seceded. And even upon completion of his moral crusade, he still did not see Blacks and whites living together as equals.

# White excuses

Perhaps one of the biggest problems with the founding fathers is that they have inherently given white Americans a built-in excuse for being delusional and making terrible political decisions. Many of the paths I crossed on my journey through political science took me to places where I could witness the conditions of poor whites, especially in the South. However, having grown up in the Pacific Northwest, which had its own pockets of rural poverty inhabited by whites, in addition to their fascination and admiration for the Confederacy, although Oregon was neither in nor anywhere close to the southern Confederacy was dumbfounding. I can assure you that the conditions and undeterred ignorance and delusion suffered by poor whites were not exclusive to the South. I have this argument constantly in class with my students when discussing the intersectionality between race and class. What inevitably pushes race over the edge in any discussion about the role of race versus class in the material conditions of Black people in America is undoubtedly the role and conditions of poor whites. I remember reading Thomas Frank's *What's the Matter with Kansas?* and Rick Shenkman's *Just How Stupid Are We?* and feeling relieved that I was not the only one witnessing the sheer stupidity that permeates American society, much of that stupidity is exhibited by white people and with whites constituting the overwhelming majority in American politics, it was only fair to direct most of the attention toward them. How many whites have I encountered and endured where all other elements and socioeconomic data being considered, I was certainly in a higher bracket than the whites I was interacting with, and yet despite all of the objective evidence to the contrary, they did not question for a moment that they were better than me and that I was lucky to be in their presence. That whiteness, in and of itself, is all that it takes for even the lowliest, poorest, and most ignorant white person in America to believe that he is better than any Black person despite differences in wealth, class, education, or location. We have the founding fathers to blame for this.

Due to this badge of whiteness, we now have a faulty political system incapable of changing at the pace of history. This is primarily due to white America's inability to confront the issue of race in America with any resemblance of genuine accountability or authenticity. Many of my best attempts throughout my life to reason with white people on the most genuine, rational, and intellectual level quickly turned into "shut up, n*gger" or "this is how the founding fathers intended it to be" the moment they were confronted with indisputable contradictions with the racist, white supremacist thinking at the root of the American founding and of what they thought America stood for. With these two statements, the white people I encountered were able to defeat any argument that I could come up with, despite any and all evidence. And those unwilling to even engage in any discussion about institutional racism and the discrimination faced by Black people in America were able to ward off further discussion by leading off the discussion with one of these comments.

What was additionally glaring is that even when racial disparities are obvious or Blacks experience violence due to white domestic terrorism, white people have been allowed to inflict conditions upon another group of people that they would never tolerate for themselves. Throughout much of the dialogue surrounding police brutality and the murdering of unarmed Black people in America at the hands of police officers is the suggestion that "if Black people just did what they were told, they would still be alive." Despite the inaccuracy of this statement, for which there is not much that cannot be almost immediately refuted by the countless examples of whites being granted the opportunity to swear, point handguns, and literally get in fistfights with police officers without any of them feeling like their lives were so threatened to the point that they felt the need to shoot the person. Clearly, there are two sets of rules in this country when it comes not only to the political standing of Black people in America but what is expected from them when encountering the police and what role the police play in establishing "safety" in communities. Now, where would people get the idea that there were two separate sets of rules for Blacks and whites?

The founding fathers created the conditions which make it virtually impossible for Blacks in the US to attain any equitable level of equality and justice as that which is enjoyed by whites. Perhaps one of the most prevalent experiences throughout my career from student to professor is the duality of the perception of being either an affirmative action or exceptional Negro. That's it. That is where I found myself placed on the professional spectrum throughout my career, at any and all levels. Even now, my social media is filled with whites who suggest that the only way that I got my PhD and a job in higher education was due to affirmative action. This ultimately allows them to devalue my work ethic and my accomplishments by suggesting they were a handout based on race and had nothing to do with actual skill and determination. On the opposite end are those who feel like I must have been extraordinary because they had never encountered a Black person who spoke so well and knew so much. If I was not the typical Black person whom they were used to seeing or interacting with, then there must have been something special about me that made me unlike the "others," so their logic goes. Having to be perceived as extraordinary to be worthy of interacting and working within certain circles and networks certainly does not benefit the individual and certainly not the majority of Black people, who are undoubtedly considered among the parameters of the "others" that whites are used to interacting with, that would normally under no circumstances find themselves in the rooms and restaurants that I would sometimes find myself. The polarity that situates Black people as either "handout hires" or as "exceptional Negroes" leaves little room for nuance and for the majority of Black people in America to acquire any meaningful justice or equality.

# Ignorance as white virtue

The final theme that undoubtedly permeates my lived experiences as a student and teacher of political science, that can be attributed to the original act of ignorance and hypocrisy of the founding fathers, is the inability to demonstrate or voice any disdain or critique of America without being told to be grateful, or that if I did not like America, then I should just go back to Africa. As a student of political science and, certainly, as I chose to make its study into a career, I have certainly leveled a considerable critique of the founding fathers and many, if not all, of the social, political, and economic institutions found within American politics. Having previously been declared inferior, coming from an uncivilized, barbaric, dark continent, certainly I had no right to complain about the racism and constant injustices that we, as Black people, encounter in our daily lives. The audacity to believe that, as a Black person, I should just be grateful for the privilege to interact with whites, even the poor, avowedly racist ones, is the height of delusion that resonates within white America. No matter how poorly treated or dilapidated our material conditions, surely we are better off for having been enslaved and ultimately civilized by whites, despite their constant rejection and threats of violence. Seriously, how can Black people in America be expected to compete with such flawless logic? It's almost as if white people have an answer for everything!

My problem with the founding fathers is that they created an institutional framework that made it impossible for Black people to attain justice or any resemblance of equality in the US. They eliminated any reasonable dialogue between the two races by arbitrarily declaring one inferior in mind, morals, and character, and thereby enabling the other to forego any respectable attempt to govern and participate in the American experiment. For democracy to work, it requires a minimal level of unity and practice of equality within the community that allows one to govern and to be governed by others. Democracy cannot survive with one portion of the population openly despising and oppressing the other, and yet, the history of this American experiment is rife with political inconsistencies of this sort and institutional racism.

# Conclusion

What are Black people left with? At every point of my lived experience, there are the constant roadblocks and inevitable confrontations with the racist, white supremacist thinking of the founding fathers. Every argument made by the founding fathers is still found within the basic framework of white political thinking in America today: Black people were not meant to be equal participants with whites in the American republic. It is not what the founding fathers had in mind, and the majority of white Americans know this. And yet, here we are, trying to force racial equality within a system that was built purposefully on the inequality of the races. America only works if one group oppresses the other. Perhaps that is what the founding fathers had in mind from the beginning, hence the idea that once inevitably freed, the formerly enslaved should be returned back to Africa. The founding fathers left us with a faulty, failed experiment and no peaceful, reasonable way to fix it. And no one seems willing to hold them accountable.

# 4

# I'm no politician or elected official

There are many professional roads to take with a degree in political science. Although I made up my mind fairly early that I wanted to be a college professor, I still needed to test the waters in state and local politics early on. Between my bachelor's degree and returning to graduate school, I flirted with Washington state politics. When I graduated from Howard and moved back to Portland, again, I considered a career in politics. Even after getting a taste of teaching, there was something about the art and game of electoral politics that I found interesting. Overall, each time I was tempted to test the political waters, I was reminded of how frivolous and incompetent American electoral politics is.

With a degree in political science, there was potential there for me to be a great politician. First, I would learn the inner intricacies of the discipline and how the institutions work. Knowledge of elections and American politics should make a person more electable and a better elected official. It seems that there is a pretty direct connection between the two. Second, even if I did not have the face or temperament for it, I could be one of those behind-the-scenes strategists who come up with all the great ideas that somebody much more polished and better looking then used to win an election. I was good at debating and charismatic when I wanted to be. At the very minimum, I could be a speechwriter for some politician on the local level.

Growing up, I never knew or read about any Black politicians or elected officials. Most K–12 education focused on Martin Luther King, Jr (MLK) and Rosa Parks, neither of whom were elected officials, despite their national notoriety. The first Black person that I can remember running for office was Jesse Jackson back in the 1980s. His message of "keep hope alive" was based on the idea of creating a Rainbow Coalition, which was futile, although it was catchy. By the end of his failed attempt to win the Democratic Party's nomination for president of the US, Jesse and his "keep hope alive" was more of a caricature mocked on late-night television and in Black culture.

A few years later, it was Al Sharpton's turn to take a crack at the Democratic Party's nomination for US president. Like Jesse before him, he attempted to be a racial uniter, speaking to the fears and misplaced resentment of middle-class, white America, while trying to covet poor, working-class whites. Also, like Jesse, Al's claim to fame was that he was a student of MLK and used his status as a reverend to attempt to literally walk in the footsteps of MLK. He had a very non-threatening message that was sure not to turn off middle-class white Americans, and he appealed to the moral fabric of Americans by carefully weaponizing his church upbringing to advocate for racial harmony. Like Jesse before him, Al also had no chance of winning and did not get very close at all to securing the Democratic nomination. Two of the most respected and prominent Black men in the community and neither one of them had a chance of winning the party's nomination and certainly not the national election. I remember wondering during those times what the point of them running was. This was the late 80s to early 90s; America had yet to have any racial justice awakening that gave any impression that the country was ready to have a Black president. Were they doing it for show? What exactly did they hope to accomplish running these meaningless campaigns for a position they had no chance of winning? This was my first experience with the symbolic gesture of politics.

Although I definitely did not know of any Black elected officials who were then currently in office, there was Clarence Thomas, but he was appointed to the Supreme Court. The most I can remember about his nomination process was the disparaging treatment of Anita Hill and the backlash within the Black community following his confirmation. Sure, Clarence Thomas was Black, but he was the wrong type of Black person. He was a conservative who was being nominated by a Republican president. The optics were terrible. No one in the Black community I encountered, or interacted with, considered Clarence Thomas to be a significant representation of the Black political community. If anything, he symbolized everything that was wrong with it. This was my first experience of understanding that just because you were Black and in a position of power, this did not mean that you were interested or invested in bettering the lives of the Black community. My mother always used to say, "all skin-folk ain't kinfolk." She was talking about Clarence Thomas.

My own experience with running for any type of office ran out when I was in high school. The first office I ever ran for was in elementary school, where the students essentially took turns being class president. Although it was a democratic process, essentially a class vote done by paper ballot, the position was pretty much meaningless. That being the case, I lost. There was no platform or significant speeches to be given. The class president did not get to make any big decisions other than being in front of the line when we left the classroom. The whole concept of having class elections in elementary school appeared to be nothing less than a lesson in the democratic process. No wonder I still am not a fan! To my classmates' credit at the time, I had a reputation as a bully and received my fair share of behavioral referrals and out-of-school suspensions. Most students in my class had previously witnessed my violent outbursts at some point and thereby had a certain understandable level of fear. Nevertheless, that fear did not carry over into the democratic process because I had lost a symbolic, meaningless election.

I decided to take a break from student government until my sophomore year in high school. Two of my best friends and I had decided that we were all going to run for student government for no better reason than to spite the traditional status quo in which the same ol' people had been running and winning the same offices over and over for years. We just got tired and frustrated with the phony and symbolic "leadership" of student government. It was not just our class, but the student government had essentially not changed from one year to the next, outside of the incoming freshman class. Why were we voting for and electing the same types of people every year when there were basically no changes in the material conditions of our daily lives on campus? Was student government all about organizing assemblies and having pizza parties? If so, as a student who was getting bored in the classroom anyway, that sounded like a pretty good gig if you could get it. Clearly, I was not presidential material. Therefore it was decided that I was going to run for secretary while the other two ran for president and vice president.

Collectively, we had no agenda; we were just anti-establishment. Unlike my elementary school experience, this time there was a speech that was given to the student body during an assembly. All the candidates for each office were required to give a speech to the student body about why they should be elected. When it was my turn, I didn't have anything written down, a trick that I still use to this day. Having watched a lot of historical documentaries about the world's greatest dictators and military leaders, I had a pretty good idea of how to give an engaging political speech. I waved my arms and pumped my fist as I argued how there was an unfair hierarchy in school that favored the privileged and popular kids. By this time, I had taken up playing golf a few months before and had tried out for the high school golf team instead of playing baseball as I had before. Playing off the lack of attention and notoriety of my new spring athletic home, I declared how I would stick up for the sports that received no attention, like the golf team. By the end of my speech, there was the perfect amount of laughter and applause to provide enough confidence to leave the assembly with my head held high. When the results came in and news spread that we had won, I felt better about having thrown a wrench into the smug, stereotypical high school routine than I did about actually doing anything as the class secretary. Similar to elementary school, the position was mostly symbolic, and there was no grand school policy or agenda that we were advocating for or trying to implement. I was comforted by the tears of the students whom we had beaten in the election.

It felt good to just win if, for no other reason than everything that I despised about high school, for at least one moment, I was able to claim a small, although insignificant, victory. That year the senior class had elected a Black male as their class president. He was a soccer player whose dad was a cop who was known for harassing the other Black kids in the neighborhood. He fit right into the stereotypical, non-threatening mold that would enable him to get elected class president. Not to mention the fact that he dated a cheerleader at the time, which made his win seem like it was something right out of mainstream 80s popular culture. Once I was elected class secretary, I felt for that brief moment that someone from the outside was finally going to take a seat in a meaningless, symbolic class government. Needless to say, my stint as junior class secretary was short-lived.

That one experience in a meaningless class election provided me with enough lessons about American politics to sustain me to this day, and as a teacher I try to share it with my students whenever possible. Sure, the rich kids had more money and more opportunities, they were more popular, and they lived in better neighborhoods, but there were more of us than there were of them. In the end, if we all banded together under a common theme with a common cause, we could still exercise enough power to win when we needed to. You had to have the right message, and you had to have the right messenger. The key to a successful politician was the proper mixture of both. Appearance would only matter at the surface level. For most people, politics is about what you can do for them. If you did not look the part, you could still win with a strong, charismatic, and enthusiastic style that spoke to the spirit of the downtrodden. They were the majority! They just needed someone who was unafraid to speak like them and for them. Someone who didn't care about trying to fit in and who had some experience of being rejected, and who was not one of the stereotypical kids who lived up on the hill. The masses always had power when democracies were involved. That is the gift and the curse of democracy. If the people are wise and united, they can protect themselves from the wealthy elites who look to take advantage of them. But if they are fractured and ignorant, they end up fighting themselves more than fighting those who are actually responsible for their misery and deplorable conditions. The people had to be at least capable of recognizing their own fates if nothing else. As the candidate, it's your job to motivate and inspire the people. It is very theatrical. With the right message, even the worst politician could win an election. But a good politician with a good message could really bring about change. The problem with all of this is the nature of democracy. I could not compete.

## What about a career in politics?

During my junior year in college, I decided it was time for me to get a job that was a little more fulfilling and provided a lot more real-world experience in a field I was interested in. After two years, it was time for me to do something else besides working in the fitness center collecting student IDs and studying. It was a work-study position that paid very little but was very easy to do, and most of the other people who worked there were student-athletes, and the majority of people that visited the fitness center were student-athletes. Most importantly, there was a laundry facility on-site for the staff to wash and dry the gym towels, which provided the perfect opportunity for a poor student like me to do laundry for free. Unsure of any academic future, my backup plan was going to be to work in government in some way. Having no network to rely on, the best thing I could do was go to the university's work-study office and check the job board for availability somewhere else. I had brought my car up from Portland and had finally moved off campus into my own apartment, so the idea of working off campus felt right.

The first thing I realized about being young and Black working in politics was how ill-prepared I was. Not mentally or emotionally, but materially. Prior to college, I did not own one suit, nor did I know how to tie a tie. I had never been to an occasion special enough that required me to wear a collared shirt with a sports jacket. When I went away to college, I was required to wear a sports jacket and tie on away trips while traveling with the football team, so my mother and I scrambled to Burlington Coat Factory to get me something to comply with the team's dress policy. To work in a government office daily, I was going to be required to wear a tie and jacket daily! I was poor and owned only one jacket. Ultimately, I had to spend what little money I had to get as many 3 for $19.99 tie and shirt combinations as my work-study salary could buy. Not to mention shoes. I did not want to come off looking poor and unprepared. It felt so typical of a young, Black male working in a government office: wearing the same suit over and over again but switching out the shirt and ties that everyone can notice. I did not want that to be me, so I spent everything I had trying to "look" the part. Everything was worn and discounted, but I was able to put just enough together to look like I belonged.

My first job in government was with the Washington State Attorney General's Office Consumer Protection Division. The Consumer Protection Division in Tacoma, where I worked, is composed of attorneys and professional staff. The division enforces the Consumer Protection Act and helps keep the Washington marketplace free of unfair and deceptive practices. The main goal of the division is to investigate and file legal actions to stop unfair and deceptive practices, recover refunds for consumers, seek penalties against offending entities, and recover costs and fees to ensure that wrongdoers pay for their actions. Division staff participate in the many legislative initiatives that affect consumer protection each year. The division's Consumer Resource Center provides an informal complaint resolution service. The informal complaint resolution process includes notifying businesses of written complaints and facilitating communication between the consumer and the business to assist in resolving complaints. The Consumer Protection Division provides information and education to businesses and the public on consumer issues and issues alerts and press releases to warn consumers and businesses about fraudulent or predatory activities.

The Consumer Protection Division offers an informal complaint resolution service to Washington State residents and to consumers with complaints about businesses located in Washington State. Through this process, they contact businesses to determine their response to consumer complaints. If a business refuses to respond or to make an adjustment, it cannot compel them to do so. They inform consumers of alternatives if the complaint resolution service is not successful. The Attorney General's Office is authorized to bring legal action only in the name of the State of Washington and is prohibited from serving as an attorney for individual consumers. Consumer Protection Division staff are further prohibited from giving advice, rendering opinions or interpretations, or conducting research on behalf of individuals or businesses.

My work in consumer protection was at a call center for people to complain about a business. The office had a variety of predetermined template letters that we would send out to businesses informing them of the complaint. When we were constantly filling up envelopes, we were being yelled at by people all over the state who wanted to complain about Best Buy not honoring their 30-day money-back guarantee. There was absolutely no executive power or authority for anyone in that office to do anything to help these people. The other half of the floor on which we worked was full of lawyers who worked on cases for the attorney general, but we never interacted with them nor had any idea what they were ever working on. Our last line of defense to make the people feel better was to threaten to report the business to the Better Business Bureau, and you can imagine how well that went with people who had spent a significant portion of their income on a used car, only to find out it was a lemon. For some reason, they were not comforted by the fact that we would be sending a stern letter to the used auto sales lot with a pamphlet on lemon laws.

Besides getting a first-hand glance at the ineffectiveness and inefficiency of local government, the best thing about that position was that all of the other staff that I worked with were college students as well, and some from the neighboring college Pacific Lutheran. Between taking the occasional phone call, the majority of the time was spent talking and debating sports and politics while stuffing envelopes. Since I was at the peak of my willingness to express and argue my newfound political identity, the office was the perfect arena to practice. I was the only Black person in the office, so it helped to be aware of the consistent basic critiques that I would receive when trying to explain to my white coworkers how capitalism and democracy were hurting Black people. Two of my colleagues were conservative, and I enjoyed talking with them about their positions and why they felt the way they did. Of course, they were mostly oblivious to the conditions experienced by Black people, but I was more curious about how they were able to perceive the world in the way that they did. What I found is that we agreed on more things than I thought. I had my fair share of criticism for Democrats, and together we shared moments laughing at their incompetence.

When I left there, my next stop was the Washington State Commission on African American Affairs. The Washington State Commission on African American Affairs (CAAA) serves as the official state representative of the African American community—advising the Governor, Legislature, and state agencies regarding policy development and implementation. The Commission also works to establish relationships with local governments and private sector organizations that promote equal opportunity for African Americans. The Commission has one paid executive director and one paid executive assistant who work full-time for the Commission. The Governor appoints the executive director, who serves at the Governor's pleasure. The Commission also has a nine-member volunteer Commission Board appointed by the Governor.

After my stint at the Consumer Protection Division, I was excited to be put in a position where I could research and work on the politics that directly impacted Black people. This is what I got into politics for! The position was unpaid, but that did not matter. By this time, I was just hungry for the experience and to get a glimpse of what practical, local politics in the Black community looked like. Most of the time, I was doing research from home, tracking bills from across the state, and checking their progress through the legislature. The Commission's nine members had specific bills from their districts that they were responsible for monitoring in the hope of being able to influence legislation that impacted Black people across the state. Twice a month, I would travel to the office and meet with the director to provide a summary of how things were moving through. Since I had just finished my degree, I was eager to utilize any moment I could to offer a few suggestions and ideas, and it was the first time that I occasionally felt heard. Unfortunately, the Commission had an advisory role to the Governor only and had no voting or executive power to actually implement anything. Our suggestions could go completely ignored, but the Governor liked having us around. I got a glimpse at the issues that directly affected Black people but still had no access to the actual decision-making mechanism that was vital to make political change.

My next stop in working for government, again, came with the Washington State Legislature, but this time for the Washington State Senate and Senate Committee Services. Senate Committee Services provides professional, nonpartisan research, fiscal and policy analysis, and administrative support services to each member of the Washington State Senate and its committees. This is accomplished by:

- Providing information and analysis that is objective, accurate, and useful;
- Assisting senators in developing and evaluating legislative options to achieve their policy objectives;
- Drafting clear, understandable legislation that accomplishes intended objectives;
- Facilitating committee meetings and other legislative processes; and
- Supporting opportunities for organizational and personal learning to ensure that staff have the knowledge and capability to provide senators with high-quality service.

I was appointed to the Senate Committee on Agriculture, Water, Natural Resources & Parks. This committee considers issues relating to agricultural production, marketing, and sales. The committee looks at water issues, including water levels and municipal water use. The committee has oversight over matters relating to fish and wildlife, as well as mining, forest practices, and forest fire protection. The committee also considers parks and recreation, issues relating to aquatic lands, and the management of certain state-owned lands.

After my year with the Commission of African American Affairs and gaining a first-hand glimpse of the issues impacting Black people, I still had no experience with the voting and legislative process, much like working in Senate Committee and at the Attorney General's office that were similarly detached from Black issues. The committee on Agriculture, Water, Natural Resources & Parks had no Black committee members and did not address any issues that were important to me or that I felt were important to Black people. Again, I was the only Black person on the staff, and I was very disappointed that I had been given the assignment to work on the Committee on Natural Resources & Parks. I was hoping for something a little closer to home that I was actually interested in and passionate about. My disappointment did not end there. Once I got over the initial excitement of walking around the state capitol of Olympia, walking through the chambers, and watching votes from the stands up above, the monotony and routine of day-to-day government set in and, once again, I was confronted with the fact there was very little engagement nor immediate concern for the issues affecting Black people. Black people never came up in any of the sessions or meetings I sat in. There were few Black representatives on campus, and none of them were on my committee. I sat through meetings and committee votes on dog parks and whether or not to allow dogs in restaurants. I didn't own a dog, nor did I see why this was even an issue worth taking up government time as if it were a pressing issue that the people of Washington State could not do without. Certainly, there were bigger, more important issues for which the state legislature should be spending its time crafting laws, and I could not understand why they did not spend the bulk of their time on those issues. I remember thinking to myself on many occasions: THIS is exactly why things don't change.

The last position I held in government was in Washington DC as an intern for the Consumer Specialty Products Association (CSPA). The CSPA is the premier trade association representing the interests of companies engaged in the manufacture, formulation, distribution, and sale of more than $100 billion annually in the US of familiar consumer products that help household and institutional customers create cleaner and healthier environments. CSPA member companies employ hundreds of thousands of people globally. Products that CSPA represents include disinfectants that kill germs in homes, hospitals, and restaurants; air fresheners, room deodorizers, and candles that eliminate odors; pest management products for home, lawn and garden, and pets; cleaning products and polishes for use throughout the home and institutions; products used to protect and improve the performance and appearance of automobiles; aerosol products and a host of other products used every day. Councils like the Federal Government Relations & Public Policy Advisory Council and the State Government Affairs Advisory Council identify key state legislative and regulatory issues affecting CSPA member companies and develop positions and strategies to help advance policies that support industry interests. Positions developed by the councils are used for formal meetings with policymakers and for testimony used at hearings.

My position with CSPA was similar to my bill-tracking experience with the Commission on African American Affairs in Washington State. I have no idea why I thought national politics would be any different from local politics. Even more than the nostalgia I felt walking around the halls and chambers of the state capitol in Olympia, Washington, the halls, and chambers of the nation's capital felt more important. So many important people had walked those halls that I had only seen on television. Once again, I found myself tracking bills that had little to nothing to do with Black people or Black politics, but it was a very valuable experience to track bills and watch politicians maneuver on the national level. There were always issues that directly impacted people's lives outside of the Black community, and it was valuable to experience politicking on those issues as well. It made more sense why issues concerning Black people were so hard to legislate and implement. Just like at the local level, there were pressing issues nationally that directly impacted Black lives that I was much more concerned about and interested in. Gentrification and national health care were two huge topics and concerns in the Black community at the time, and it did not appear to me that much was being done at the national level to address these issues and when they were addressed, Black people were talked about as being somehow detrimental to or having a negative impact on the possibility of the legislation being well-received. At the national level, just like at the local level, Black people were an afterthought of the legislative branch. If this was the primary chamber with the ability to address the political needs of the Black community, Black people were going to remain frustrated.

# Conclusion

To conclude, to say that I was disheartened by my experiences working in politics would be an understatement. Throughout much of my early life, I was always told that the best means by which to improve the conditions of the community is through democratic government. Black people no longer had to take to the streets in protest or threaten violence to feel empowered and improve their material conditions. Since the end of the Civil Rights Movement gave way to the Voting Rights Act, Black people in America had a new strategy to advocate for racial justice and to improve their status and standing in America. And yet, the way that American government and political institutions are structured, Blacks' ability to manufacture material gains that close the social and economic gap with whites has remained elusive. Based on my experiences, the frustration that many Black people have with the ineffectiveness of American politics to provide racial justice is justified.

Much of the underlying feeling that I had working in politics was frustration. First and foremost, the community that I was most interested in helping and working for was the Black community, and the majority of the time, I found myself placed in positions where that goal could not be further from reach. In most cases, the issues I worked on were universal in that everyone in the larger community would benefit. Black people were the numerical minority and, thus, least likely to benefit from the policies being implemented. If I was going to work in politics, I wanted to work on Black politics. From the very beginning, I felt frustrated at working in a government call center. People had legitimate complaints about businesses overcharging and money missing, but the best we could do was send them some template letter detailing how we would try to reach out to the business and refer them to the Better Business Bureau. As if that was going to satisfy people's needs! One can only imagine the people who would be most likely to need the resources of consumer protection.

When I finally got involved in the politics that directly impacted Black people in Washington State, I learned all too well that Black people were to be seen and rarely heard. Institutions liked the perception that they were attempting to be racially diverse and progressive, even if they really had no intention or belief in advocating for issues that would improve the conditions of Black people. We were there to advise, and to keep the bosses informed on the issues and pulse of the Black community, but there were absolutely no means to directly influence or impact the decision-making process. What was the point of collecting all of that data to demonstrate how the current policies were negatively impacting the Black community if it was just lip service? I sat there while the state legislature debated and passed legislation on declaring the Walla Walla sweet onion the Washington state vegetable while working for Senate Committee services in 2007. Who the hell cares about that!? Is that what people actually consider to be the workings of an effective government? I couldn't believe that I was witnessing government in action, and it had nothing to do with Black people or even implementing measures to protect the poor and oppressed. No, the government was deciding on a state vegetable.

I still believe in politics in theory, but the practice of politics currently is a disaster. In many ways, I feel like it is a lot like the teaching profession. All the wrong attributes get celebrated and promoted, while all of the negative and corrupt aspects of the practice go unnoticed and ignored. Additionally, politics, like teaching, is a skill. There is a particular art form and rhythm to being a great politician, especially in democracies where your ability to get elected is left in the hands of the people. Just because you can get up there and recite the predetermined party line on mainstream political issues and get elected does not make you a good or effective politician. Similarly, just because you can stand up in front of the classroom and click through a PowerPoint presentation and grade exams does not make you an effective teacher. There is a dance of engagement that stirs up the people or students that makes them want to be better constituents. If I couldn't change the world in politics, I could definitely change the world through education.

# 5
# The professor

After years of dejection from experiencing and watching the political process in action, the next best thing was to be a professor. I must object when people say those who cannot do, teach. It was not that I could not be successful at a career in politics, either as an elected official or a staff member for someone in office. Rather, I became completely dissatisfied with the political process as a viable option to make the political, social, and economic changes that I felt were necessary not only for Black people in America but for American society overall. The art or skill of politicking was an everyday occurrence as a young Black male in a predominately white field, located in mostly predominately white areas, and saturated with predominantly white ideas. It was not all about "shaking hands and kissing babies," although a certain amount of public pageantry came along with higher education. Nevertheless, more importantly, it was about navigating the political and racially hostile environment and still getting what you want to progress and move forward. If anything, after leaving politics as a career, I felt even more confident and empowered in my political abilities, but for what? Ultimately, I realized that my abilities and what I can bring to the table can have a much more significant impact somewhere else, and that is in higher education.

Remember, I always wanted a career where I could bring about the most change and improve the material conditions of Black people. Where I once thought that the justice system and then running for office were the best ways to accomplish my goals, it had become clear that being a teacher was where I could do the most good. My decision-making power as an elected official would at most be one voice in a democratic process with very little influence. I had seen people with great ideas and political intentions being drowned out by other senators, other committee members, and people with absolutely no sincere interest in solving the problems of Black people, let alone those of poor people. I had seen great ideas that had the potential to solve real-world problems for the majority of people in an area get shelved and not passed through a committee in favor of passing a state onion bill. It did not provide the kind of direct involvement that I wanted to have in political discourse.

As a professor, there was a greater chance for me to make the changes I wanted. First, I could continue to read and think and theorize. I wanted to be a problem solver, which required the freedom and leisure to think, philosophize, and generate ideas without many constraints. It would also allow me to write and publish ideas that would outlast my lifetime. Although I had somewhat reconciled with my spiritual and religious beliefs, I still had to hold on to a sliver of realism that admitted the possibility that we could be wrong, there is no heaven, and that what we do in this life is all we have. If that is the case, living forever is only accomplished through our works while alive. Thus, I may not live forever, but just as I had evolved through college by engaging with texts written a thousand years ago, and by reading, and analyzing the political theories of Black theorists from 100 years ago, my ideas could long outlive my physical existence. Moreover, although my ideas may not make the immediate impact I hope for, making a valuable contribution to the discourse leaves the potential for some enthusiastic scholars to stumble on my works many years from now. Just think about it, a political decision may only last an election cycle, but my words and ideas could last forever.

Outside of the practical reason that university professors have the opportunity to secure a job for life through acquiring tenure, for someone who had just experienced the extreme lows of poverty and homelessness, the idea of a permanent job was highly tempting. I had also had enough of the typical nine-to-five work schedule. Over time, I realized that it did not work for me, and the idea of being trapped in a workspace for a designated time gave me anxiety. The intermittency of hour classes with breaks to decompress and regroup before doing it all over again was a much better work environment for me. Over the years, camping out in libraries and sleeping in my van produced a somewhat sporadic and unpredictable writing and research pattern. Sometimes I read and worked ahead. Ideas came to me at all different times of the day, and I had gotten used to sleeping with a notepad in case I wanted to write down my thoughts or ideas while I was waiting for the streets full of college kids to quiet back down for me to get some sleep. The freedom to work whenever I wanted was too good to pass up and, as a professor, I could do this.

The university also provided ever-flowing, non-stop access to ideas. Access to books and research by colleagues at other colleges and departments on campus allowed unlimited access to ideas and, more importantly, intellectual discourse. I would be surrounded by the exchange of ideas and discourse on various topics, and I could always find something new to learn about. Working on a university campus in a college town reinforced the idea of my being a student for life. Furthermore, this would keep me young in thought and never too out of the loop with current events and social events in the community, even if I rarely participated in them myself. College was full of 18 to 25 year olds, and just by walking around campus and witnessing the pageantry of college life, it was possible to feel the youthful energy that vibrated through college campuses. How could I feel old, surrounded by so much young vibrancy and inquisitiveness? Thus, teaching became not only a mutual exchange of ideas but also an exchange of energy and ideas: I would provide a framework to explore their intellectual curiosities and, in return, they would provide me with the energy and vigor to continue to teach and passionately engage in political discourse.

Additionally, being a teacher allowed me to cast the widest net possible. Every six months, there would be a new batch of students with new perspectives and potentially fresh ideas. There was the opportunity to retry old theories on new students and constantly be amazed when new questions or problems were brought up in later semesters. The students would have different backgrounds, majors, passions, and motivations. While I was getting older, the students were getting younger, leaving the potential for the ideas and concepts discussed in class to take on a whole new meaning for a different generation. Although higher education has been overcome with the ills of capitalism, such as for-profit institutions that treat students as customers and not vessels to be filled with knowledge to make the world a better place, it was still possible to reach those students who wanted to be reached. There was the opportunity to work with graduate students and engage with special topics one-on-one. I could see myself as the Socrates to a young and upcoming promising student, playing the role of Plato. The thought of helping someone else achieve their own intellectual and academic goals was the type of service that I was inspired by. Having the opportunity to lead someone into a career or introduce an idea that would captivate and lead them through the exploration of their own beliefs and personal identity that I had experienced as a student, was at the root of what I felt the role of a teacher should be and one that I particularly took seriously. I could interact and engage with 50 to 100 students during one semester. Over time, that would put me in direct contact with thousands of students. Again, although higher education was not the bastion of intellectual wealth and advanced thought that I had hoped or believed was its traditional purpose, I knew that even in the midst of wealth-seeking capitalists, there was still the possibility of reaching a few students to make it all worthwhile. Among the barrage of students who just wanted to get their C and get the hell on with their degree and those who saw a good grade as nothing more than a grade point average tied to their tuition, it only took one intellectually curious student to keep me hopeful. Sometimes while trying to reach everyone, you end up reaching that student who sits in the back who has quietly contemplated many of the themes and concepts brought up in class and just has been waiting for someone to engage with them in a discourse about what they're thinking or experiencing. Those students can make an otherwise insufferable class the most meaningful.

Teaching politics was the best fit for me, not because I was studying it and most qualified to teach it at the university level. Since graduate school, I had gone beyond traditional political science into much more profound depths of Black Studies, including African history, religion, and philosophy. This growing level of knowledge started to supersede my daily reading and intake of the traditional political works and drew me to topics that included Black liberation theology and the history of social movements. I remember reading *The Mis-Education of the Negro* by Carter G. Woodson while I was attending Howard University and immediately felt responsible for the craft and pursuit of educating Black people. The thesis of Dr Woodson's book is that Black people of his day were being culturally indoctrinated rather than being taught in American schools. The most imperative and crucial element in Woodson's concept of miseducation hinged on the education system's failure to present authentic Negro history in schools and the bitter knowledge that there was a scarcity of literature available for such a purpose because most history books gave little or no space to Black people's presence in America. Some contained casual references to Negroes, but these generally depicted them in menial, subordinate roles, and as more or less subhuman. Such books stressed their good fortune at having been exposed, through slavery, to the higher (white man's) civilization. There were included derogatory statements relating to the primitive, heathenish quality of the African background, but nothing denoting skills, abilities, contributions, or potential in the image of Blacks in Africa or in the Americas.

Woodson considered this state of affairs deplorable—an American tragedy—that doomed the Negro to a brainwashed acceptance of the inferior role assigned to him by the dominant race and absorbed by him through his schooling.

The universities were full of history courses that covered the Black experience. There were courses in sociology and English that examined racism and social inequalities that, although not necessarily specific to the Black experience, did provide small and mostly impartial glimpses into the history and experiences of Black people in America. Although Puget Sound had only a small department with a minor in African American studies, across the country there were thriving, fully funded departments specific to the Black experience that were available for students to tap into. Yet, I did not recall any specific department or field that catered to the Black political experience. I had questions: where did Black people learn about politics? Where did I learn about politics? My friends and family certainly did not engage in deep, meaningful discussions about political affairs or parties. I do not recall my parents ever advocating for one political candidate or another or sharing their party affiliation. The social studies books of my youth certainly never covered Black people from a political standpoint other than slavery and its political implications and always from the foundation of white people as saviors who were just trying to do the best they could to create and maintain a nation based on the principles of freedom and equality, despite the brutal torture and violence they perpetuated on Black people. If there was any area that I felt Black people needed to know and learn more about than anything, especially for the purposes of liberation and improving the experiences and material conditions of Black people in America, it was the political process. Our oppression and history of racism, disenfranchisement, and the resulting pathetic social and economic conditions Black people have found themselves in have been political in nature. It was essential to share this.

# Breaking ground in the classroom

The first time I got to teach a class of my own was during my second semester of graduate school, filling in for Dr Ring's feminism class. Since I had been granted a fellowship, I was assigned to her as a grader, which meant I attended all of her classes and followed along with the readings. It was the first time I had been introduced to the readings of bell hooks and Michelle Wallace, and I would use their theories to argue against the male domination of Black leadership and the road to Black liberation in my thesis. Until then, I had never conducted a class alone, and this one was not even mine. But I kept with the readings and occasionally engaged in the class discussion with the other students, so there was a comfort level that would allow me to lead a discussion as a graduate student. There were so many questions about women and feminism that I had during the class. However, because I was sitting in and not enrolled in the course, I was not 100 percent comfortable asking questions and felt it more necessary to let the students paying for the course take the lead. However, since I had the opportunity to lead the discussion, I was going to make the most out of it.

I remembered an episode of the Boondocks about the trial of R. Kelly. The Boondocks was an adult-themed cartoon sitcom that focused on a dysfunctional Black family, the Freemans, settling into the fictional, friendly, and overall white suburb of Woodcrest. When the trial of R&B singer R. Kelly comes to town, the radically different brothers Huey and Riley are on opposite sides of the trial. During the trial, R. Kelly's attorney questions a witness about being urinated on by the artist, to which she replies that if she did not want to get peed on, she would have just moved out of the way. Although the students laughed, at the end of the episode I informed them I was trying to make a point about the issue of women's equality. We all debated and discussed the back and forth between the young lady and the attorney. Even the few males in the course who generally surrendered any controversial position to the women in the classroom felt emboldened enough to comment. After the class was over, a few students stuck around, and we continued to laugh and discuss a few of the comments and ideas that were said in class until it was time for the next class to take over the room. As I walked back to the library to study afterward, I felt intense satisfaction and energy flowing through my body. I felt like I could run a marathon. If I was going to teach, I knew I needed to repeat whatever I did that day.

By the second year of graduate school, I had been assigned as a discussion leader for a western civilization class with over 100 students. To allow students to discuss and ask questions about the readings in a class that size, the department broke them into three separate discussion sections that students were required to take. As the discussion leader, I was also responsible for grading. This would be the first time I would be responsible for determining another student's grade. The readings were already predetermined, and the professor had already lectured on the material, so it was my job to get the students to discuss it. Some issues were more controversial and led to much livelier discussions than others. By then I had built up a wealth of stories, personal anecdotes, and many theories about the human condition from many angles and was unafraid to provide my personal opinion on topics. I found that students engaged more when I had some personal stake in the game by offering my opinion on the subject matter and then letting them argue with me.

My views, rooted in a personal philosophy that was far from traditional, had me taking stances and taking the side of dictators and villains of western civilization and American history. The issues were not even necessarily centered around race. We read Frankenstein and Martin Luther's Reformation, and in each turn, I argued the most controversial stance with passion because I sincerely believed it. Similar to my first opportunity to lead a discussion, the post-class discussion was sometimes better than the discussion that took place in class. Students stuck around to ask even more damning and controversial questions, and we argued back and forth. It was only a short time before the class spent half of our section time discussing the readings and the other half arguing about current events or trending social topics. Seeing the opportunity to introduce topics not covered in the readings, I experimented on the students with my theories. Again, the success or failure of the discussions depended on the rapport I built with the students over time. As long as nobody had received an atrocious grade that was completely unwarranted, students were content to come and argue with me and each other for an hour twice a week.

At that point, I only had one theory that I had researched and investigated since I was an undergrad student. I called it my 95/5 theory. The concept came from my foundational theoretical frameworks regarding leadership and the human condition from Plato, Aristotle, Machiavelli, and Nietzsche. All had a very realistic and somewhat skeptical perception of humans and argued that the great and exceptional man in any community was few and far between; the masses, overall, were sheep, blinded by their passions and fueled by emotionalism and, rarely if ever, basing their actions on reason or intellectual exercise. As a result, there should be no surprise that the country's political, social, and economic standing was poor and gross. Just look at the condition of the masses! I had no exact name or number just yet. Still, in my math class as an undergraduate student, my best friend and I at the time would consistently joke about the empirical rule in statistics regarding calculating standard deviations. The 68–95–99.7 rule is a shorthand used to remember the percentage of values within an interval estimate in a normal distribution: 68 percent, 95 percent, and 99.7 percent of the values lie within one, two, and three standard deviations of the mean. The values within one standard deviation of the mean account for about 68 percent of the set; within two standard deviations account for about 95 percent, and within three standard deviations account for about 99.7 percent. When either he or I were at our philosophical peak during class or among our friends, we would joke that we were always three standard deviations of truth when we were speaking, basically signaling that, when at our best, we were always right. 95 percent had a great ring to it, and I thought that fewer people would find it offensive. But 99.7 percent was too high a figure, leaving very few people in the population to carry the mantle of greatness. Plus, 99.7 was not catchy enough. Thus I engineered what came to be my "95/5 Theory," which argues that 95 percent of any given population is ignorant. In contrast, only 5 percent are capable of unselfish reason and rationality that allows them to lead the masses who are incapable of leading themselves to a good society or government. I had kept notes and had been working on this theory since before I left Tacoma. My experiences wandering around the Nevada desert, being homeless, and sleeping in my van gave me time and motivation to feel invincible in the face of adversity. And now, as a discussion leader, I have a captive audience and the perfect opportunity to try my ideas and theories out on other people.

The next time I had the opportunity to substitute lecture for my adviser was in her introduction to political theory class. I decided to scrap the discussion of the readings for that day altogether and brought the notepad that had been beside me in the van where I slept. Before getting started, I notified the students that we were going to try something new that day and asked that they follow along. Then I opened up my flimsy spiral notebook and went through my 95/5 theory on the board. As I got through my first point, that 95 percent of the population was ignorant, the students started to laugh and gripe. The hands started to go up, but I told them to hold off until I had written the entire theory on the board, and then I would take questions, and we would discuss it. By the time I had finished, damn near every hand was up, and rather than wait to be called on, students started yelling out their questions and dissatisfaction with what was being suggested about society and the human condition. Who was I to call people ignorant? What made the 5 percent so special, and why should anyone listen to them? I argued back passionately, pointing to the board. By the time class ended, I was out of breath. As people were leaving following the end of class, two students stuck around and kept talking as I packed up. As we were walking back to the department where I now shared an office with another graduate student, the Black female student who was in the class and following along remarked that she had never seen a class like that before. "And you know what," she said, "you're right. Most people are ignorant as hell." When my adviser returned to class the following week and asked the students how the class had gone, they were up in arms about this "damn 95/5 theory" that the graduate student had shared last class. When she and I met later that day, she mentioned how the students couldn't stop talking about it and that I had made quite an impression on some students. I knew it.

I have studied the great theorists and political speeches of presidents and dictators throughout history. All the authors and theorists I admired had a unique voice and style of their own that drew the reader in, and I wanted to have the same thing. Plato read like having a conversation; Machiavelli read like reading a lawyer or an accountant, providing very specific and direct examples; and Nietzsche and Marx read like they were yelling, that the information they were sharing was so extremely valuable that they wanted to be sure to have the reader's attention. I couldn't wait to use an exclamation point in one of my papers.

Although I had my own theories, it was essential to have a teaching style of my own. I wanted to be the type of professor that I had always wanted when I was in college: someone who cares about the topics and subjects that they teach. The type of professor that did not just tell students what to think but allowed them to learn to think about the concepts and explore them on their own. Someone who did not just sit there and talk at the students but who engaged with the material and talked with the students. I was highly attracted to the dialectical method I had read in Plato who used his teacher and mentor, Socrates, to tell his stories. The push and pull, back and forth between teacher and student; the asking of questions and pushing students to investigate why they hold the beliefs they do and come to the conclusions that they do. As a student, I recall that nobody bothered to ask the simple question: why? Because that is how I was raised or was always taught. Yet, now, not asking why was no longer acceptable in political or philosophical discourse at least not the way I understood it. You had to provide sound reasoning or evidence for holding on to such firm beliefs or to taking political actions that had consequences for the community. As a student, I wanted to argue and debate with the material and the other students in my courses. Students should be able to challenge the ideas and beliefs of other students. Too often, I recall not having had the opportunity to challenge many racist and ignorant comments that my fellow students had said in class. That is how the classroom could be a vehicle for change— through the mutual exchange of ideas with an added level of accountability through discourse. All ideas were acceptable and could be offered on the table, and any existing idea could be challenged no matter how old or popular the belief was.

The first real chance I had to actually teach a credited course from beginning to end came after I moved to Washington, DC and joined the political science department as a PhD student. Unlike my experience at the University of Nevada, I started out my graduate career at Howard University with a research fellowship that once again paired me with my adviser to grade papers. By this time, being a college professor was my only mission and goal, but there were no opportunities to teach a discussion section of a much larger course similar to what I had done at Nevada. The department was smaller, and I did not foresee any upcoming openings that would get me in the classroom at Howard. Having my master's degree already meant that I was eligible to teach classes as an instructor at the community college level. So after my first year in the PhD program at Howard, I decided to look for teaching experience elsewhere. There were many colleges in the area to choose from, but Northern Virginia Community College (NOVA) in Alexandra, Virginia decided to give me an opportunity in their department of political science. As an instructor in the political science department, I had no office, just an office computer in a cubicle that I could use to make copies. As the new instructor, I was given the bottom load of courses that were left over after all the full-time and part-time faculty had chosen their courses.

Perhaps nothing prepared me more for teaching political science than my experience at NOVA. In my two years there, I taught everything from the introduction to political science class to classes on Congress, political ideologies, and the US presidency. Having to teach such a broad range of political sciences courses gave me confidence that I would be able to teach anything. I was certainly no specialist on Congress or the US presidency, but my years of knowledge studying US politics and the American government had given me enough tools, in addition to the book and course readings provided by the class, to be effective. I taught summer courses, in addition to teaching during the fall and spring in between teaching my own courses at Howard University. NOVA was a good 45 minutes and two trains away from my apartment on the northeast side of DC and yet another two separate trains from NOVA to get to Howard. So on the days when I had to teach at both institutions, I would take two trains sometimes just to teach one 50-minute class, turn around and take two more trains to teach another 50-minute class at Howard. I did all this under a very strict time frame, where any slipup or missed train could leave me anywhere from right on time to 20 minutes late. But there is no doubt in my mind that this was the best experience overall in preparing me for a future in teaching. I had to be prepared to teach a variety of topics within the discipline, which I thought would be helpful in setting me apart when it came time to get a job.

Teaching a variety of courses outside my expertise was beneficial in regard to showing my training in traditional political science and my ability to teach basic courses that would be found at every university in the country. These courses provided nothing to scratch the itch of Black liberation politics and my passion for merging the two. But by now, the education I was receiving at Howard enabled me to slowly introduce concepts from outside mainstream political science and incorporate more and more Black politics into my courses at the community college. Slowly but surely, I was turning these classes into my own.

One thing that made my introduction to teaching political science easier at NOVA was that most of the students were around my age, and on a few occasions, I had students who were older than me. At the prime age of 30 years old, I was still pretty hip. But I also had an old soul from my parents that enabled me to reminisce about the good ol' days with some of the older students. Having been on a college campus for the previous eight years had left me somewhat current so I was still able to identify with many of the younger students. Not having a car also proved to be beneficial because it gave me the opportunity to stay and converse with students after class on days I wasn't sprinting to the bus to get back across town to Howard. An important tool that I remember from my days at school in Nevada was accessibility. Being accessible to students would help with my ability to relate to them as well. Being able to relate to students, especially when you are new, makes teaching a lot easier. I started to develop a routine with how I taught these classes. For each class, I would try to start out with a current event or something light just to generate conversation. Sometimes these conversations would completely take over the class. We could be 30 minutes into what happened over the weekend before someone would remember that there was a lecture topic for the day that we were not getting to. Normally, this might not sit well, but it opened up the conversation to everyone, and it opened the door for students to get to know me better personally. Accessibility matters.

When you aren't afraid of the students falling asleep and the students feel like you care about what they have to say, the job is a lot easier. Just as in my earliest lecturing days, after class is when a lot of the deeper, more impactful conversations would take place, and because I had no car and was in no rush to go home, there were many times I would just hang out in the classroom until the next class was about to start or until the conversation had run its course. Also, because the bus ride to the metro before taking two buses could be very taxing, there were many occasions when I would walk to the TGI Fridays nearby and have lunch with students or with whomever had time in between their own classes. It wasn't long before a group of us were routinely meeting over lunch and drinks to have loud, rambunctious conversations about politics and the state of the human condition.

One of the best and most eye-opening experiences in my teaching career came during my second year at NOVA. There was an entire international cohort of students from Sweden and Norway who had enrolled at NOVA as part of their study abroad experience. The vast majority of these students were political science majors or interested in international politics and diplomacy for their careers. As a result, a lot of them ended up taking multiple classes with me. This was my first real interaction with international students and my first time having them as students. For most of them, it was their first time being in the US, so it was a great opportunity for us all to learn. They asked a lot of questions about Black Americans and American culture outside of what they had seen on television. I asked a lot of questions about Black people and where they were from, but there weren't many. Like many of my students, I was also the first Black professor that they had had. I still keep in touch with many of these students today. Some have returned to the US and gone ahead to graduate school. I truly had the opportunity to teach any and everyone. They tried to show me some of their customs, and I tried to get them to eat chitterlings, a staple in the Black community during the holidays, especially for Thanksgiving. Our closeness in age and the passion and confidence with which I taught and shared my ideas with them made the experience unforgettable.

One of the things that is key to engagement in my classroom is not just dictating to the students and leaving them with more unanswered questions but being open and available to offer a perspective of your own. There was a lot going on in Washington DC at the time, with the Obama administration taking office and with the then Vice President's wife Jill Biden taking a teaching job at NOVA while she was in Washington as well. While our nation was debating Obamacare, they had come from countries where universal health care was the norm. A lot of American politics did not make sense to them. Hell, it did not make sense to me either and to hear it from international students who were experiencing it for the first time, definitely made me feel better about my cynicism.

The greatest benefit of my early teaching days at NOVA was not just the type of classes I was given but how many. I went from teaching one class, one day a week, as a graduate student in Nevada, to teaching three classes, two days a week. It was a memorable crash course in class preparation and organization. In addition to teaching multiple classes back-to-back on completely different subjects, it was also my first time having to create my own assignments and tests. I had to create writing prompts and be responsible for tracking and monitoring student grades. But most importantly, I had to develop and fine-tune the art of teaching. It is very important, and I tell students and colleagues this all the time now, to have a teaching style of your own and, like every other skill, you have to practice it. There are not any courses or graduate classes on teaching. No one ever sat me down and gave me a quick tutorial on how to teach or develop college courses, create assignments, or grade papers. I learned all of these tools through observing my advisers and by trial and error. The same kind of assignments that my advisers had used for their undergraduates, I was now using.

Since I was still in school myself, I had little time to research and create assignments of my own, so I saved time by mimicking the same style of assignments that I was used to. I quickly learned to organize and create PowerPoints for my lectures and utilized a flash drive to get from class to class, without missing a beat. I learned what to teach. Not a lot of people talk about this when discussing getting into the teaching profession. A lot of education has become the reciting of names, dates, and formulas, and it's convenient for a teacher to concentrate on those for the students. But what I learned about studying political science at Howard is that there is more information on a topic that can be covered and retained by students in one undergraduate-level class. Names, dates, and formulas may come in handy for a test or to pass off as general knowledge, but those things do not put students' butts in course seats and do not get them to come back to class. There has to be more than that if you want students to engage in the material and look forward to coming back. Names, dates, and formulas are easy to teach and even easier to find. What I gathered from the experience was that students were much more interested in little-known historical facts and alternative theories to preexisting and unchallenged knowledge. Teaching students the difference between how senators are elected versus members of the House of Representatives is fine.

Students should certainly know that I might put it on a test, and no one teaching about Congress or US politics should neglect to teach these concepts to students. However, I have learned that what gets students to think critically is more nuanced subjects like how many Black people or women have been in Congress, or why the senators were not directly elected to office until more recent history. How and why things work is just as important as merely describing what things are. Talking about the average age of elected officials and the differences between young and old voters are the type of discussions within the context of learning about Congress and the legislative branch that help students engage in the material.

Most importantly, teaching at NOVA gave me more opportunities to sharpen and fine-tune my teaching craft. I tell my students and colleagues all the time that anyone can sit at a desk or behind a podium and lecture. But teaching, the art of transferring knowledge from one person to another in a classroom, is performance art. The students are there for 50 minutes to an hour, and they expect you to entertain them. When you walk into that classroom before class starts, you're on. The "camera" is rolling, and every gesture and word that you speak after that moment is officially on the record. You have to act like an authority figure but not tyrannically. They won't believe you if you sound and act unsure about the content or what you are teaching, so you have to command a certain presence of authority in the classroom yet still be warm and friendly. But sometimes you have to be tough and mean to students as well. Nothing prepares a person more for engaging in politics in regard to character and temperament development than teaching higher education. These students are adults. They don't have to show up. There's no bus dropping them off, and there are no parents to whom to send report cards. Education and grades for many students are a business, and they see themselves as customers getting a service that the college or university is providing. Most of the time, they don't care if you're having a bad day or not feeling great. Your significant other could have just broken up with you, or you could be struggling to pay the bills, and the students will be right there waiting for you to teach them, and they will expect you to be on point and engaging every time. You can have a huge impact on a student's life and future career, but you can also deter a student from pursuing higher education or wanting to get involved in your discipline just by taking your class. It is quite a responsibility. Practice may not always make perfect; in fact, being the perfect teacher may not even be possible, but it can certainly make you better. There is no doubt that my first teaching experiences certainly made me better. I had every opportunity to practice and refine my teaching skills as a graduate student, and this was an invaluable experience.

## Officially on the market

By the time I left Washington, DC, I was so confident that it would not take long for me to get a job. By the time I completed my PhD in political science, I had many years of teaching experience in a variety of concentrations within the discipline. Not only did I have experience, but political theory and American government were core specializations within the discipline that were taught at every institution. Not to mention that I had a rare and distinct specialty that, thanks to the Obama presidency and the nation's current fascination with racial politics, had started to appear on more and more job boards within the discipline of political science. I always kept note of the phrasing in job postings and highlighted sections that mentioned or emphasized the candidate's ability to contribute or bring something unique or different to the table that was not currently in the department; I was certain I had that with my specialty in Black politics and research interests in Black political thought. Throughout my dissertation writing process, I had always kept a separate manuscript version from what I had defended and successfully submitted it to a publisher that offered me a contract. I continued to attend academic conferences and gain teaching experience. When it came to thinking about my prospects of getting a job, I felt more confident and ready than I had ever been. I had a book ready, teaching experience, and a unique and thriving research interest. What could possibly go wrong?

By 2016, I had been on the job market for three years looking for a full-time position. I was on the job boards daily, looking for any possible job in either political science or African American studies. I had complete job dossiers for both disciplines. There was no part of the country that was off limits. I even applied for a job in political science at the University of Montana! In the meantime, I could no longer afford to live in Washington, DC, so I had to move back home to Portland with my family. To make a living, I went back to teaching at the community college level, and before you knew it, I was driving back and forth across town between Portland Community College, Mt Hood Community College, and eventually Clark College in Vancouver, Washington. Once again, I was teaching everything from introduction to political science to international relations. Being an adjunct instructor provided no job security or assurances of employment at all. Each semester I waited for the full-time faculty to choose their courses, and if there was anything left over, then I would be given whatever course was left. So there were some semesters when there would not be anything available, and I would be stuck on the outside looking in. When there was no availability in the classroom, I had to take construction jobs. With literally no experience, I started waking up at 3 a.m. to build walls in the mall and clean up construction sites. At night I was coaching high school football at nearby Milwaukee High School. In just a two-year span, I had applied to over 121 jobs in either political science or African American studies, for everything from full-time tenure track positions to visiting professorships. By 2016, I was 0 for 121 with only a handful of interviews.

I made the most out of every opportunity I had to get back in the classroom. While at Mt Hood Community College, I became involved in the Black Student Union (BSU) as the faculty adviser and started working with the other Black students on campus to bring awareness to the conditions Black people face on campus and in the community. When the semester ended in May of 2016, I received the instructor of the year award. By the summer of 2016, just a few short months later, they no longer had any room for me. I was out.

That August, I was preparing for another season of football and construction when I got an email from the University of Missouri asking if I was still interested in a job that I had applied for back in January but had not received a response from yet. I replied that I was definitely interested but found it slightly odd that they were still hiring for someone to start in the fall when it was already a week into August. The opportunity was for a two-year postdoctoral student that would be jointly appointed in the departments of political science and Black Studies. A postdoc is a person who conducts research after the completion of their PhD The ultimate goal of a postdoctoral research position is for the student to pursue additional research, publishing, or teaching in order to have better skills to pursue a career in academia. Although there were no assurances that my two-year appointment would turn into something afterward, it was no secret that there was a hope that this position would turn into a full-time joint appointment between the two departments. Initially, I could not think of a better fit. I was given the opportunity to do political science AND Black Studies at the same time! It was like a dream come true. The interview took place on Thursday with the chair of Black Studies and a representative from the Dean's office and the department of political science. The interview took place via Zoom, and I remember having to wake up early to get ready because of the two-hour time difference. When it was over, I had no more confidence than I had previously had for any of my other interviews. By this point, I had been on a couple of Zoom interviews, and they all seemed to end the same way except for one at a small college in Illinois. The chair of the political science department there was actually very interested in me, and we had spoken a few times over the phone. When we decided to make plans for me to visit the college, he wanted to confirm with the director of graduate studies in the political science department at Howard that I was indeed at a point in the program where I was a viable candidate for the position. The next day after talking with the graduate director, the job was pulled, and the college expressed that they were no longer interested in me as a candidate. I was not too surprised due to the incompetence and fragile ego of the faculty members that I had left behind. For years they had touted and advanced mediocre talent at best and barely anyone who could certainly qualify as an intellectual. All of their "talent" ended up taking government desk jobs and working locally. So when I was no longer under consideration for a job in Illinois, I was grateful because, once again, I was getting the opportunity to succeed on my own merits without having to squabble and brownnose incompetent faculty that had recently become completely irrelevant in political circles and surely had no reputation to speak of that condoned such inept and incompetent behavior. Thus, when the University of Missouri reached out, I knew this was the chance that I had been waiting for. A few hours after the interview ended, I got a call from Mt Hood Community College to inform me that they were receiving calls from the University of Missouri. By Friday morning, the chair of the department of Black Studies called and offered me the job and wanted to know if I would have any problem being ready when classes started the following week on Monday.

By this time, I had already made the decision in my mind that I was going to say yes, no matter what. Classes were starting on Monday, and I had exactly one week to find a place to live, pack up my belongings, and move to Columbia. On Monday, the university provided a letter of employment for me to give to a management company for housing. I had spent the entire weekend on Craigslist looking for a place to live, although I had no idea about the area or what was a safe environment. All I knew was that I wanted to be close to campus but away from students and student housing. By Tuesday night, I was on the road driving from Portland, Oregon to Columbia, Missouri, with my car hitched to the back of a U-Haul. I had literally interviewed, accepted the job, and drove 2,000 miles in a matter of a few days.

Prior to moving to Columbia, I had never been to Missouri outside of passing through on one of my many cross-country travels on vacation. The most I could remember was the arch in St Louis. Missouri had been heavy in the press recently, beginning with the Ferguson protests. The Ferguson, Missouri protests began with the murder of Michael Brown, an 18-year-old Black man who was shot and killed by police officer Darren Wilson on August 9, 2014. Brown, who was college-bound and had no criminal record, was unarmed, although local police accused him of robbing a convenience store moments before the shooting. The shooting almost immediately triggered protests in the St Louis suburb, as demonstrators took to the streets to speak out against what many saw as yet another example of police brutality against young Black men, for which Ferguson has a troubling record. The situation subsequently escalated and drew national attention when police reacted to protesters, even those acting peacefully, with military-grade equipment, such as armored vehicles, tear gas, rubber bullets, and sound cannons. Tear gas was used in combination with rubber bullets, smoke bombs, and flash grenades to disperse crowds of protesters.

One of the major demands of protesters was to get prosecutors to put Wilson on trial for the Brown shooting. But a grand jury decided to not indict Wilson after three months of deliberations— in what many saw as a deeply flawed, biased investigation led by local officials with close ties to law enforcement. The unrest reached a breaking point when on November 24, 2014, the grand jury reached the decision not to indict Wilson on any criminal charges. Many of those waiting outside the Ferguson Police Department grew violent and the situation intensified. Multiple buildings were torched, and protesters hurled rocks at parked police cars. This continued into the following day when Missouri Governor, Jay Nixon, deployed the National Guard and reinforced law enforcement presence in the area, effectively bringing the protests to a stop.

On September 12, 2015, a Facebook post by the student government president, Payton Head, described bigotry and anti-gay sentiment around the college campus, which gained widespread attention. He claimed that in an incident off campus, unidentified people in the back of a passing pickup truck directed racial slurs at him. The first student protests occurred on September 24, 2015, at an event called "Racism Lives Here," where protesters claimed nothing had been done to address Head's concerns. On October 24, a police officer responding to a property damage complaint reported that an unknown vandal had smeared feces in the shape of a swastika on a bathroom wall in a dorm on campus. The University's Department of Residential Life filed photographs of the fecal smear in a hate crime incident report, and the residential life director emailed a number of people on campus. On November 3, student Jonathan Butler launched a hunger strike, vowing not to eat until president Timothy Wolfe resigned. One of Butler's stated reasons for this was that Timothy Wolfe's car had hit him during a protest against Wolfe at the school's homecoming parade. Students confronted the president by linking arms in front of his vehicle. The car revved its engine and following this Butler was bumped. On November 7, with hundreds of prospective students flooding Mizzou's campus for the university's recruiting day, student protesters intervened with a "mock tour" where they recited racist incidents that occurred at MU, beginning in 2010 with the dispersion of cotton balls on the lawn of the Gaines/Oldham Black Culture Center, along with more recent events such as the use of racial epithets against two young women of color outside of the MU. student recreation complex. On November 8, university football players announced that they would not practice or play until Wolfe resigned, potentially costing the university a one million dollar fine if they had to forfeit an upcoming game against Brigham Young University. The Southeastern Conference Football Commissioner issued a statement saying, "I respect Missouri's student-athletes for engaging on issues of importance and am hopeful the concerns at the center of this matter will be resolved in a positive manner." The Mizzou Athletics Department previously indicated that it fully supported the players' actions.

The protests attracted widespread local, regional, and national news media attention. Some protesters said the coverage was impacted by journalists' lack of previous race-related experience, reliance on scripted behaviors, and a desire to cover the event as "outsiders looking in." Wolfe issued a statement on November 8 implying that he would not step down and that he was "dedicated to ongoing dialogue to address these very complex, societal issues as they affect our campus community." On November 9, however, Wolfe announced his resignation. Later that day, Chancellor Loftin announced he would resign at the end of

2015 to take a research role at the university. His departure was hastened by the Board of Curators on November 11.

The NAACP began circulating a travel advisory after the state passed a law that Missouri's NAACP argued allowed for legal discrimination. The warning cites several discriminatory incidents in Missouri, including examples of "looming danger" in the state. "Individuals traveling in the state are advised to travel with extreme CAUTION," the advisory warns. "Race, gender, and color-based crimes have a long history in Missouri." The advisory was issued after Senate Bill 43, which makes it more difficult for employees to prove that they're a protected class, like race or gender, directly led to unlawful discrimination—this was passed through the Missouri Legislature in June. Missouri Governor Eric Greitens signed it into law soon thereafter. The advisory aims to make visitors aware of a string of troubling events in Missouri. In May of 2016, an African American man, who had never been arrested, died while being held in jail. Threats of violence and discrimination had gone unaddressed on school campuses in the state, the NAACP said. And a 2016 report from the State Attorney General's office found that African Americans were stopped by traffic officers 75 percent more often than Caucasian drivers, a rate disproportionate to their makeup in the state's population.

All of this was taking place against the backdrop of my arrival on campus. Friends and families called and wanted to make sure I knew what I was doing when they heard the news that I had taken a job in Missouri. My mother was initially worried about my safety, of course. My friends kept wondering if I had been keeping up with the news and the hostile environment for Black people that was being made public at the time. There were many friends asking "are you sure?" when I told them where I was going. But I had waited far too long for this opportunity, and there was no way I was going to turn back now.

# Conclusion

When I first got to campus, I remember being amazed at the mere size of the university. I was not sure where to park on the first day, so I ended up by the football stadium, over a mile away from where I needed to be on the first day. Since it was a joint hire in two departments, I was given two offices, one in each department. From the very beginning, I felt more at home in Black Studies. For one, I was not the only Black person in the department. Second, on one of the first occasions of meeting another faculty member in political science, I remember being asked what I specialized in and responding, political theory and Black politics. His response to that was, "oh, so you're an activist scholar?" It was at that moment that I knew I was entering into an intellectually hostile environment. When I scrolled through the department faculty pages again to see all the white faces that looked alike and studied the same things, I decided I was going to spend the majority of my time at Black Studies. Since I was getting a late start on campus and they didn't have a class for me yet, I was given the first semester off from teaching and was able to focus on carving out some research first while I got acquainted with the area and campus. The beauty of it was that I was given free rein to create a class of my own that I wanted to teach, an opportunity that I was more than ready for. I had already gone through the trouble of creating my own Black political thought specialty that I planned to introduce to both departments. The first step was to create a Black political thought class.

Since I was brand-new to campus and no one knew who I was, I created a flyer to advertise my course, which I taped outside the door to my office. For the design, I used a blackened silhouette of myself as the main image, with a short course description underneath. A week later, I got an email saying that political science was not happy with the flyer and they did not want it posted outside of my door. Of course, I left it up. They had made it more than clear that they had no interest in what I was doing or what I was bringing to the table. By the second year, I was on the docket to teach my Black political thought class, and with only my flyer and no name recognition at all, the course was made with over 20 students in it. For a class to "make," a minimum of 12 students have to register for it to avoid cancellation. As a newcomer, for my class to not only make but to get 20 students was big for me. In addition to Black political thought, political science had given me an American government course to teach as part of my one-to-one teaching commitment.

When my two years were coming to an end, political science informed me that they would not be looking to keep me in the department as part of the joint hire with Black Studies. In fact, they wanted the department of Black Studies to commit funds to bring in another person from the University of North Carolina to have my job. Fortunately, I had made my impact with the students and within the department of Black Studies and they decided to bring me on as a full-time tenure track hire, solely in their department. Political science went on to hire their person but with no commitment from Black Studies. A year later, that professor left for another job at Oklahoma. There has not been another Black faculty member in the political science department since.

# 6
# Conclusion

War is described as a conflict between political groups involving hostilities of considerable duration and magnitude. It is a struggle or competition between opposing forces for a particular end. What this reading represents is my own war with politics, political science, and academia. In my life, a number of political forces operate: my own individual Black identity, which is complex and developed over time, the white dominant majority among whom I was raised and went to school with throughout most of my childhood and academic career, and then there is academia as its own separate institution, which functions as its own political identity. There is a standard, certain expectation to be met, where radicalism is discouraged, there are relationships and social conditions to maneuver and massage, and there are cultural norms and mechanisms to punish and isolate members of the academic community which leaves many within the academy to carefully navigate their research interests and publication record in order to not fall out of the institutional norms. Thus, the end that these opposing forces are vying for allows one to feel at once empowered in one's Black identity and capable of using politics to change the material conditions of one's community, and also defeated as the other espouses anti-Black racism and looks to limit the political power and effectiveness of the Black community.

The conflict is between my ability to investigate and nurture an empowering sense of self and Blackness in an environment that is hostile to both who I was as a young Black male and who I hoped to be as a Black intellectual and political scientist. It has been a lifetime of open hostility toward a goal of unapologetic confidence in my sense of self as a Black American without any political leanings or political affiliations, but very hostile to the political status quo as established by the founding fathers in the US. How do I express confidence in being pro-Black in a community, on a campus, in a department, or in a country that completely devalues Black contributions or sees little worth in the historical experiences of Black people?

In many instances, the society and the specific environments in which I found myself in higher education and in politics were based on confinement, restraint, and limitations. You can never be too Black, or too smart, or too anything in one way or another. The last thing that you are suggested to be is your authentic self. How do I highlight the political history and experiences of Black people in the US and across the diaspora when the discipline in which I find myself has no interest in investigating or sees little value in the political identity and experiences of Black people? And one that consistently falls back on the founding fathers and the Constitution as the birth of this country to do so, as if either emerged independent of the political identity and experiences of Black people. This war has been going on my whole life.

To say that writing this manuscript was challenging is an understatement. There were so many things to consider. As much as most of my experiences can be perceived as doom and gloom, they all bring me a considerable amount of joy today. Although

I never go out of my way to share my experiences of becoming a university professor, there was something therapeutic about reexamining how I ended up in the field I am in now, at the university where I currently teach.

Ultimately, I would like to believe that everything happened for a reason, and I have no doubts that I would not be the intellectual or the teacher I am today without all the trials and tribulations of my academic career, no less than in my personal life.

Thinking back to my days as a student, there are so many things that I would have done differently, considering the roller coaster of an academic career that I have had. In the beginning, I wish I had had more courage and confidence in being book-smart. There is a lot of conversation in the Black community around this idea of rather having street smarts versus book smarts, and the notion that there is something lacking in the book-smart person's ability to maneuver through the rough and rugged Black community. The idea that Black people who read, watch documentaries, are being "nerdy" or "acting white," is one of the biggest cultural and societal issues that harm the Black community the most.

There are a lot of things that Black people do that could easily be negatively viewed as acting white: being a supportive fan of Clarence Thomas, being a Republican and showing up at Trump rallies, believing that racism no longer exists, and that Black people have an equal chance in this country with whites. But the notion that reading and being book-smart somehow detracts from one's Blackness and thereby be perceived as "acting white" by some in the Black community is an atrocity. I wish I had done a much better job of navigating that space growing up. Perhaps this is what people mean when they talk about the significance of nurture in a person's development because, perhaps, I would have done a lot better job of navigating my social spaces if I had had a Black educator or intellectual to help guide me early on. At the same time, I do not want to completely ignore the facts of my own decision-making that most likely played a much larger role in my ability to navigate social spaces while in school. There was nothing or anyone forcing me to deny or attempt to downplay "book smarts" in order to fit in with a crowd and society that would eventually reject me anyways, and one which I would also grow to despise in my own right. W. E. B. Du Bois is famous for his concept of double consciousness when explaining the experiences of Black people in America. The term represents a challenge African Americans experienced of "always looking at oneself through the eyes" of a racist, white society and "measuring oneself by the means of a nation that looked back in contempt." The term also referred to Du Bois's experiences of reconciling his African heritage with an upbringing in a European-dominated society. There is no doubt that I felt this growing up and throughout much of my academic experience. But, perhaps internally, within the mind of a Black intellectual, there is another psychological war going on inside that takes place due to the conditions within the Black community. These conditions have consistently put the Black intellectual at a significant disadvantage of having to cope with the experience of being looked at as foreign or a representation of the oppressive race by members of their own community. What a disadvantage it must be to have to hide one's intellectual prowess consistently and steadily or always have to dumb down your language and vocabulary when talking to friends or roaming the halls at school. The isolation that comes with having to retreat back into one's own universe, void of close friends and interaction, just to spend brief moments within a satisfying intellectual playground. You essentially become two Black people in one, depending on the circumstances and conditions.

The problem comes when there is no viable outlet for young Black people to express their intellectualism without being socially punished for it. What can be worse at a developmentally peak socialization stage than to have your peers believe that you're acting white based on your intellectual abilities? It has the power to make you not only shy away from your immediate intellectual talent but reject any future attempts at exploring and advancing your academic curiosities and pursuits. Looking back, I despised having to "act cool by acting dumb." These two things should never be mutually exclusive, and yet, growing up, I saw and experienced too much of this. Being unapologetically smart needs just as much attention and promotion in the Black community as promoting natural hairstyles. My inability to accept this challenge early on played a significant role in my relationships with other Black students and friends of mine until I went to graduate school. It was an extreme disservice to myself and to the other Black students at my high school to have to navigate the psychological landscape taking shape so poorly within me as a young student. I was a very poor leader, and I feel partially responsible for the negative experiences of many of my Black friends from high school. Today, I try to express my hope for younger generations when it comes to Black intellectualism and decrying intellectualism as "acting white" as much as possible.

But it would be wise not to come down too hard on myself, because the part of my double consciousness that had to interact with the larger white community took precedence at certain moments in life. Navigating predominantly white spaces as a frustrated and angry young Black male is as much a matter of survival as anything else. Throughout my academic career as a student, I never felt as though I was entirely free. There was always some constraint on my abilities to move and think freely. Trying to navigate when and how to portray a certain level of Blackness that would enable me to express myself completely while also not doing any harm to my ability to walk the halls, enter the classroom, or walk around campus without any problems. If I had known then the trials and tribulations that I would suffer later on as an undergraduate and then as a graduate student, I would have been a lot more courageous in navigating my Blackness in predominantly white spaces and institutions.

I still think that politics is a viable way to make significant changes in the material conditions of Black people in America. Looking back, as much as I like to lean on my philosophical foundations, I wouldn't change anything about my academic path and what I decided to concentrate on. It would be nice if I saw more Black students taking political science courses. The field is just as important in understanding our conditions and experiences as history, sociology, or criminal justice. In many cases in the Black community, young people need to see someone in that career before deciding to pursue something similar. I would like to think that my position in higher education will assist some young Black scholars in developing an interest in studying politics. Even now, there are very few Black students on campus interested in political science, and I have been sending more and more graduating seniors into law school or graduate school in other departments like sociology or psychology. Perhaps this may be due to the fact that political scientists have not done a very good job at relating to the public, and most of the Black pundits you see covering politics on TV have a background in journalism or criminal justice.

American politics is heavily reliant on the founding fathers. The problem with the founding fathers is mainly that no one holds them accountable, and mainstream political science refuses to criticize their debauched experiment. Throughout my entire academic career, as both student and teacher, I have yet to encounter the proper amount of contempt and criticism leveled at the American founding fathers for the political disaster that America currently finds itself in. Decreasing political knowledge and sophistication in a political system where a reasonably intelligent populace is necessary for it to function properly increases political polarization, where the extremes on both sides dominate the political conversation. All these ailments, not to mention the growing racial hostility in this country (just look at the increasing numbers of white nationalist groups), and yet no one is willing to go back and look at the origin story of the nation and take aim at those chiefly responsible for the construction of this failed experiment. There is something disingenuous about the study of American politics that appears to have completely absolved the founding fathers from responsibility for the tragic political environment we are experiencing.

My disdain and distrust of the American founding and its resulting political institutions ultimately affected my professional experiences working in politics. All of the jobs I took in politics were enlightening and eye-opening as to how politics work at the local, state, and national levels. Out of all of my career experiences working in politics, the Washington State Commission on African American Affairs was the most satisfying and fulfilling, although it may have been the least indirectly influential in the political process. It was the one most directly related to the political experiences and the material conditions of Black people in Washington State. I hated the symbolism of the institution as an adviser to the Governor without any assurances or accountability for the work that we were doing. Admittedly, I have not kept up with the local politics of Washington State outside of the protests and gentrification currently taking place in the Seattle area, but I would hope that given the current political climate, the Commission has grown to develop a closer relationship of accountability with those who can make substantiative changes to the material conditions of Black people in the state.

That is not to say that I would never reconsider getting involved in some form of electoral politics. Moving out of Portland, Oregon, which many times felt governed by electoral determinism because progressive Democrats dominate electoral politics for the most part, and relocating to the Midwest has certainly changed my perspective on state and local politics. Missouri needs a lot of help, and there are a lot of places off the "main strip" (the stretch of highway that covers the state west to east from Kansas City to St Louis, with the college town of Columbia right in the middle) that are victims of incompetent politicians and institutions that fail to improve the conditions of the people who live there. I worry about these areas and the encounters that Black people in the state will potentially have there. I was astonished to learn of white students who had yet to see another Black person that was not on the television screen until they moved into the dorms on campus. This made me wonder what becomes of the people in this state with so few encounters with people of color. What attitudes and opinions are they developing about Black people that they are then carrying over into their adult political experience? I was told when I moved to Columbia that over 80 percent of the people in the state of Missouri never move out of the state. This gives me a considerable amount of initiative to get involved politically, being that I have lived across the country and am able to bring a relative amount of experience from having lived in different demographic environments. Perhaps what the people of this state need more than anything is someone from the outside to provide a little perspective and clarity of the world outside of Missouri and Missouri's place in it. Could I see myself running for office someday? Maybe.

The election of Trump in 2016 also gave me hope for a potential future as an elected official. Not because it demonstrated how ignorant the American public was in electing someone who had no experience as an elected official and was a failed businessman whom many were inspired to vote for because he would "drain the swamp" by running the country like a business. No, I was more inspired by the fact that someone who made the type of comments that he routinely made on and off camera that were not "presidential," motivated people to vote for him because of his refreshing character in the political climate due to his tendency for "telling it how it is." If America is looking for an honest political broker, well, then look no further! For years I have been opining that the American electorate would benefit greatly from an unapologetic politician that was not afraid to ruffle the feathers of both parties in this country and really shake up the American political environment. It's long overdue! Of course, it would be nice if that person was not openly racist and called African nations "shithole" countries and bragged about being able to sexually assault women. But the political jargon has definitely taken on a different character in the last eight years, and that opens the door for people like me who may have been previously turned off by politics by having to talk a certain way. Today when people ask me about my career, and if I would rather be doing anything else, I always tell them no. I absolutely love teaching, I love being in the classroom, I love being paid to think and write critically, and there is nowhere else that I could have access to young minds while remaining as intellectually and politically active.

Ultimately, my career is not over, and there are still plenty of things I want to do. There are so many ideas and theories to share and books to write. My motivation and passion for teaching Black politics and hopefully inspiring students continues to grow. There are a lot of things that can motivate people. Two themes have consistently motivated me throughout my career: fear and revenge. Fear of irrelevancy and failure when there was no room to fail, and revenge for the widespread disrespect that I have experienced as a student and a scholar. Having been poor and homeless as a graduate student, I understand the notion that there is "nowhere else to go but up." But nothing gets me up in the morning more with the passion and fire to attack each day than the understanding that if I don't get up and get after what I want and feel I deserve each day, it's not coming, and nobody is going to give it to me. There is always in the back of my mind the possibility that I can go without eating or without a place to safely rest at night. There's nothing like the fear of going back to a hometown only to be ridiculed for having fallen short of all the hype and expectations that people had for you and to realize that you have become the one thing you never wanted to be: a nobody. There is a healthy place in the psyche for fear as a driving force to motivate someone.

Likewise, revenge and vengeance are very useful tools in the quest to overcome adversity. Similarly, they are completely healthy when aimed in the right direction, mainly toward your goals and aspirations. I have sat back while mentors and professors who were supposed to advise and guide me told me that my writing was garbage and would never be published; I watched as political science departments attempted to hire my replacement and look to promote someone without half of my accomplishments or track record; I watched departments I am associated with create opportunities and hold seminars in Black politics and excluded me while inviting outside scholars; I have been called an activist in an attempt to diminish my intellectual and academic career and research interests. I remember watching Michael Jordan's speech while being inducted into the basketball hall of fame and how he used it to thank all of his naysayers and people who doubted him throughout his career. All of this to say: there's very little that is more satisfying than proving doubters wrong. Revenge is a dish best served cold.

Today, I am exceptionally pleased with the work that I have been able to do through my nonprofit, Troublesome Movement. Troublesome Movement is a nationally recognized 501(c)3 nonprofit organization that I founded back in 2012 when I moved back home to Gresham, Oregon. Our focus is to assist in the educational attainment of minorities and other underprivileged or underrepresented populations. We are a movement that creates and transforms communities by means of political and social activism. Through leadership and education, we inspire people to exceed expectations and to eliminate the promotion of mediocrity.

The only freedom that the academy has not afforded me is the opportunity to interact and engage in the community as much as I would like to, but nonprofit work has stepped in to fill a huge void that I felt was missing. What I felt that politics could not do and where the classroom could not take me, Troublesome has been that element to connect what I try to do in the classroom with the real world. Where politics can't change the hearts and minds of people, and policy has too frequently failed those most in need, nonprofit work centered on community service and servant leadership can be an effective force of change. What's most inspiring and satisfying is that students have played a significant role in building this nonprofit, and I still incorporate students from Missouri and Oregon in our mission. In many of the arguments and debates that students and I have had in the classroom, I have challenged them to formulate solutions and have provided them with whatever means possible to devise them. Many of the activities and events that we have put on throughout the years have been entirely student driven. As its founder, I have tried to empower young people by giving them the freedom to explore their own passions while I cheer them on as a mentor, using the nonprofit as an umbrella for them to explore the problems that Black people are facing. Troublesome has been one of the most satisfying accomplishments that has come directly out of my lived experiences as a young Black male trying to make a career in political science.

There are many different paths to take to get to where you are going, and I doubt that my path is a unique one. There are also many different events and experiences that shape a person's path and motivations in life. I would like to believe that I have been blessed with the opportunities and experiences that I have been provided, although there are certain moments that I would not wish upon my worst enemies. But all of the experiences that I have covered in this text made me the academic and professor that I am today.

# Suggested discussion topics

The narrative in this book highlights the experiences of a young, Black male navigating historically discriminatory and hegemonic institutions. The purpose of the discussion questions is to give you an idea of some of the themes or concepts that are important in this work and give you a chance to explore these important topics.

1) Is there a piece of advice or wisdom that you disagreed with? Why? What would you suggest as an alternative?

2) How might you apply the author's strategies and solutions in your own life?

3) How does this book address conflict, conflicting information, or opinions?

4) What is one question you would like to ask the author?

5) Did this book change or challenge any preconceived notions you had about higher education or academia?

6) What biases do you think the author might have? How could this impact the way the book was written?

7) Which parts, if any, of the author's experience could you relate to?

8) What do you think is the most important takeaway from the author's story?

9)    What is the most important piece of advice offered in this book?

10)    Do you have any views or ideas that you think will evolve as you get older? Why or why not?

# References

Adcock, R. and Bevir, M. (2005). "The History of Political Science." *Political Studies Review*, vol. 3 no. 1: 1–16.

Annals of Congress, 1 Cong., 2d sess., March 17, 1790, p. 1560.

Bellot, Leland J. (1971). "Evangelicals and the Defense of Slavery in Britain's Old Colonial Empire." *Journal of Southern History* (February 1971).

Claybook Jr, M. Keith. (2021). "Black Identity and the Power of Self-Naming." *Black Perspectives*. September 10, 2021.

Dahl, Robert. (1961). "The Behavioral Approach in Political Science: Epitaph for a Monument to a Successful Protest." *APSR* vol. 55, no. 4: 763–772.

Dalcho, Frederick. (1832). *Practical Considerations*. Ithaca, NY: Cornell University.

Diggs, B. J. (1973). "The Common Good as Reason for Political Action." *Ethics*, vol. 83, no. 4: 283–284.

Easton, David. (1951). *The Political System: An Enquiry in the State of Political Science*. Calcutta: Scientific Book.

Fields, Gary S. and Ok, Efe, A. (1996). "The Meaning and Measurement of Income Mobility." *Journal of Economic Theory*, vol. 71, no. 2: 349–377.

Gunnell, J. G. (1993). *The Descent of Political Theory: The Genealogy of an American Vocation*. Chicago: Chicago University Press.

Hegel, G. W. F. (1967). *Philosophy of Right*. New York: Oxford University Press.

Huddy, L. (2013). From Group Identity to Political Cohesion and Commitment. In L. Huddy, D. O. Sears, and J. S. Levy (eds.), *The Oxford Handbook of Political Psychology*. Oxford University Press, pp. 737–773.

Jefferson, Thomas. (1998). *Notes on the State of Virginia*. Penguin books.

Kidd, Q., Diggs, H., Farooq, M., and Murray, M. (2007). "Black Voters, Black Candidates, and Social Issues: Does Party Identification Matter?" *Social Science Quarterly*, vol. 88: 165–176.

Leftwich, Adrian. (2004). "What Is Politics?: The Activity and Its Study." *Polity*.

Magnis, Nicholas E. (1999). "Thomas Jefferson and Slavery: An Analysis of His Racist Thinking as Revealed by His Writings and Political Behavior." *Journal of Black Studies*, vol. 29, no. 4: 491–509.

Morrison, Larry. (1980). "The Religious Defense of American Slavery Before 1830." *Journal of Religious Thought*, vol. 37, no. 2: 16–29.

Newkirk, I. I. and Vann, R. (2018). "What Black Voters Want." *The Atlantic*.

Nietzsche, Friedrich. (1998a). *On the Genealogy of Morals*. New York: Oxford University Press.

Nietzsche, Friedrich. (1998b). *Twilight of the Idols*. New York: Oxford University Press.

Padover, Saul K. (1972). *Karl Marx on America and the Civil War*. New York: McGraw-Hill, 39.

Palonen, Kari. (2003). "Four Times of Politics." *Alternatives: Global, Local, and Political*, vol. 28, no. 2: 171–186.

Paul, Diane. (1981). "In the Interests of Civilization: Marxist Views of Race and Culture in the Nineteenth Century." *Journal of the History of Ideas*, vol. 42, no. 1 (Jan.–Mar. 1981): 115–138.

Peterson, Merril. (1970). *Thomas Jefferson and the New Nations: A Biography*. Generic Press.

Rogers, James A. (1985). *Richard Furman: Life and Legacy*. Macon, GA: Mercer University Press, pp. 274–286.

Shapiro, T. and Emde, R. N. (1991). "Introduction: Some Empirical Approaches to Psychoanalysis." *Journal of the American Psychoanalytic Association*, vol. 39: 1–3.

Shaw, T. (2010). *Nietzsche's Political Skepticism*. Princeton: Princeton University Press.

Staudenraus, P. J. (1961). *The African Colonization Movement*. New York: Columbia University Press.

Walton Jr, Hanes and Robert C. Smith, and Sherri L. Wallace. (2017). *American Politics and the African American Quest for Universal Freedom*. New York and London: Routledge.

Wamba, Philippe. (1999). *Kinship*. New York: Penguin Group.

Wamble, J. J., Laird, C. N., McConnaughy, C. M., and White, I. K. (2022). "We Are One: The Social Maintenance of Black Democratic Party Loyalty". *Journal of Politics*, vol. 84, no. 2: 682–697.

Weil, Julie Zauzmer. (2019). "The Bible Was Used to Justify Slavery. Then Africans Made It Their Path to Freedom." *Washington Post*. April 30. www.washingtonpost.com/local/the-bible-was-used-to-justify-slavery-then-africans-made-it-their-path-to-freedom/2019/04/29/34699e8e-6512-11e9-82ba-fcfeff232e8f_story.html.

# Index